# *Contents*

| | | |
|---|---|---|
| *Introduction* | | 5 |
| 1. | What is Wanted | 7 |
| 2. | The Audition | 30 |
| 3. | The Interview | 43 |
| 4. | Sight-reading | 58 |
| 5. | What to Expect | 73 |
| 6. | Conclusions and Observations | 112 |
| 7. | Suggested Audition Pieces | 116 |
| 8. | Suggested Material for Sight-reading Practice | 120 |
| 9. | Three Simple Relaxation Exercises | 122 |
| *Index* | | 126 |

# Actor's Guide to

# Auditions
# &
# Interviews

Second Edition

## Margo Annett

A & C Black • London

Second edition 2001
A & C Black (Publishers) Limited
37 Soho Square, London W1D 3QZ

ISBN 0-7136-5733-2

First edition published 1995

Typeset in 11 on 12.5 pt Sabon

Printed in the United Kingdom by
Creative Print and Design (Wales), Ebbw Vale

# Introduction

This book is intended as a guide for the working actor as well as the student and those just starting out on their career. Through working as an actor myself and then as a director and teacher, I have gained considerable practical knowledge of the various processes of casting and first-hand experience of how it feels to be on the receiving end on both sides.

I came to realise how often there is a huge gap between the expectations of those involved. As an actor it seemed so hard to gauge exactly what was wanted – how to make oneself into a desirable commodity, to do yourself justice, and how to control destructive nervous tensions. It was all too easy to see those in a position of selecting actors for either professional work or drama college as omnipotent beings without human frailties or feelings. As a selector, time and time again, I watched actors courting failure with unsuitable, ill-prepared and badly presented audition material, wrestling with sight-reading or behaving in such a way at an interview that it was all too obvious that they had no idea how to handle the situation or how to present themselves. Clearly help was needed!

I decided not only to draw on my own experiences but also to ask those whose business it is to cast or provide actors with employment, to give advice and comments – on how to succeed, what not to do and what it is they are looking for.

I was aware that few, if any, actor's training courses give any tuition on sight-reading or interview techniques and allocate little time to developing the necessary skills to choose and work effectively on individual audition speeches. Feeling that these were vital to any actor, I have included specific chapters covering these in detail, together with tips on how to put them successfully into practice.

In addition, as the media have developed and expanded, the methods of casting have diversified and adapted to meet the new requirements. Even experienced actors have found themselves at a loss at castings, with little or no idea of the particular format employed or what will be expected of them – hardly the ideal circumstances in which to give of your best. I have therefore included a comprehensive section on the differing types of castings an actor might encounter.

As you will see as you read through the book, casting needn't be a traumatic experience, and although success can't be guaranteed every time it can be made more likely. And you will learn that there are a lot more people on your side than you think.

# 1

# *What is Wanted*

Actors throughout the world have one vital factor in common – in order to practise their art they need an audience. You can act by yourself for fun or as a form of therapeutic release but to complete the creative process you must communicate with an audience, however large or small.

Professional actors have to persuade others to employ them. Unfortunately these employers are disinclined to hire on trust. A straightforward, and no doubt accurate, assurance of your acting skills rarely secures a job. The employers need convincing. This is achieved through the processes of auditioning and interviewing. So many professional actors, let alone aspiring ones, are terrified of these procedures; they forget that they are for their own benefit as well as for the benefit of the prospective employer. It is the actors' opportunity to show off their talent: they are active and powerful participants, not passive victims. Without these occasions actors would be unable to meet potential employees and use them as a means of reaching their ultimate goal – the audience.

In order to get the best out of the situation it is obviously important to know as much about the proceedings as possible.

Since the advent of film and then television the entertainment business has expanded and diversified. Today the job of acting covers so much more than in the days when it referred to working purely in a theatre. The demands made on actors seem to grow daily; it is quite usual for them to audition for a commercial and a Shakespeare play on the same day. In spite of this enormous increase in the different types of work available, ironic though it may seem, the competition for it is greater than ever. It is hard for actors to find their way through the maze of different casting systems in the various branches of the media.

Nowadays, the traditional audition, where an actor is called upon to perform a prepared speech, is only one example of the ways in which an actor's suitability for a role is tested.

The interview has become universally used as an important casting method either on its own or in conjunction with auditioning or sight-reading. The interview consists of a formal chat between the actor and one or more others involved in the proposed production, i.e. the director, the casting director, the producer, the writer and all their various assistants (PAs). There is rarely more than four of these present at one time, but it can seem a formidable sea of faces to an actor entering the room. The nature of the interview depends on which branch of the media is doing the casting. An actor attending interviews for a TV film, a commercial and a fringe production will have three very different experiences.

Sight-reading has become a vital skill for an actor; it is very unusual to be offered a job, unless you are very well known, without having been asked to read from the script at some time during the proceedings.

Actors have to cope with these multifarious casting situations and it is easy to lose sight of what is really wanted especially when there are so many other actors competing for the same job.

To make their plight easier I have asked those who really know, the people who are in the business of interviewing, auditioning and in some cases handing out the jobs, to give their advice on what is wanted and what is not. They have been generous in their response. Some have encapsulated their comments in one succinct line, others have made a number of observations and then elaborated on them, but all have shown understanding and sympathy towards the actor who has to undergo the twin ordeals of auditioning and being interviewed.

## Carolyn Bartlett, freelance casting director

Carolyn Bartlett, the casting director, goes as far as to say, 'I make sure no actor leaves an interview when I am present without gaining something, even if it's only information'.

Carolyn is now a freelance casting director but for many years was Head of Casting at Granada TV, responsible for such famous series as *The Adventures of Sherlock Holmes*. She has words of comfort for actors, 'Remember, the casting director is gunning for you'. She points out that the casting director believes in the talent of the actors they put up for a part. They want them to do themselves justice and get the job. So, when you walk into the interview room you can be cheered by the thought that at least one person there is on your side.

## Wyn Jones, Head of Acting, Guildhall School of Music & Drama and theatre director

Let's go back to the beginning and look at some advice that applies to aspiring actors as well as those who are experienced. Wyn Jones is eminently qualified to offer just such guidance. He is an experienced theatre director, responsible for many successful West End productions, and is now Head of Acting at the Guildhall School of Music and Drama. He feels that casting is essentially a matter of instinct and enthusiasm. It is additionally, as he puts it, 'A question of how they respond to me, as well as how I respond to them.' He makes the valuable point that most casting comes down to a matter of taste. 'Two directors can interview the same actor and disagree violently in their opinions as to his or her talent. If you don't succeed in getting a job from one director you may easily land one the next day with another.' After those words of comfort he adds a warning. 'Jobs can be won or lost on sight-reading.'

This may sound hard but it is undoubtedly true. Sight-reading – that is, to read a script out loud with little or no prior rehearsal – has become the most usual method in all branches of the media of testing an actor's talent and suitability for a role. Even if you have performed an audition speech you will invariably be asked to read an excerpt from the script in question before you can expect to be offered the part.

Wyn then adds some further important advice: 'You'll probably get employed on a combination of your talent, looks, sight-reading and aptness for the part. You'll probably be re-employed for being generous and good to work with.'

### Albi Jones, theatre and BBC director

Another director who manages to find time to teach – in spite of a busy schedule as a director – is Albi Jones. Albi has taught at a number of major drama schools including RADA. He directs for the BBC as well as in the theatre, and established and is the director of the well respected black theatre group, Tomba. He has a passionate appreciation for text of all periods and styles. His advice is of value to all actors but is particularly worth noting if you are embarking on an audition for the first time. It concerns choice of speeches and approach to text.

Make sure the speeches you choose are really contrasting in style and context. Read the whole play through thoroughly so you know the context of the speech, the style of the playwright and as much about the character as possible. Look at the words. Notice the language your character uses. The words they choose give clues as to their attitude, personality and present mood.

## Professor Leon Rubin, Head of M.A. Director's Course, Middlesex University and theatre director

Leon Rubin is Head of the Director's Course at Middlesex University where he advises student directors on casting methods, and has also been responsible for establishing drama courses all over the world, most recently in Japan, Hong Kong and Thailand. In addition to this he finds time to work as a director in the professional theatre. Auditioning actors, he feels, has become almost second nature to him. He considers that he has developed a sixth sense for picking talent. The following are a list of his observations on the qualities he admires in an actor and what he looks for at auditions.

In an audition, I'm usually looking for intelligence, emotional truth, diversity, simplicity, analytical awareness and a sense of humour. The balance, of course, depends on the play and the character in question. Increasingly, I find myself focusing on physical movement but not necessarily technical control: more perhaps a natural elegance or balance that is difficult to describe.

Harmony of movement might be an important attribute, but I also like to see a glint in an actor's eye, the suggestion of energy and courage. It is really a gut feeling that I follow.

For actors who have left or are about to leave drama college he adds the following thoughts:

For me the audition begins as soon as the actor enters the room, even if the audition/interview isn't due to begin until later. I start to make a judgement as soon as I meet an actor, even if it's in the street. This is because many of the human qualities are as important as the technical ones. Do I want to work with this person for five weeks or more of rehearsals? I might conclude that I don't much like them, but that will not necessarily make me say no; it may be those same negative feelings that make them right for a particular character, but it is still my instincts that I'm listening to. Like me, many directors have little faith in the formal audition process and tend to lean on instinct. However, a smart actor is aware of this and begins acting the moment they meet the director.

After leaving drama college, the next stage in their career, for many actors, is fringe theatre. It is often here that actors get their first opportunity to work in the profession. However, it is wise not to underestimate the amount of competition there is for parts there.

## David Bidmead, fringe theatre director

David Bidmead runs one of the most famous and successful fringe venues, *The Etcetera Theatre* in Camden Town, London, and has the following advice for actors approaching fringe auditions for the first time.

He starts with the all important subject of CVs, photos and letters. He begs that the latter be brief, straightforward and to the point, and sent only in response to specific ads for an imminent forthcoming production. He receives about five hundred letters for each production and working through them can be a mammoth task. In the past he has been sent CVs covering several pages and long letters filled with the writer's personal ambitions and opinions on everything from the state of theatre today, to the meaning of life. Photos have sometimes consisted of family snapshots with an arrow indicating the hopeful applicant. There isn't time to wade through endless pages or peer into a photograph. It must be clear and large enough to distinguish the face at a glance, and the CV should be typed and limited to only one sheet of paper.

As for the audition itself, David, like so many directors, stresses the importance of punctuality. Time is precious. They are usually interviewing all day; if one person is late it can disrupt the whole schedule. Appearances are also important. Over-dressing for the occasion is unnecessary and it can also be distracting. That doesn't mean arriving in dirty scruffy jeans, but wearing something flattering without being over conspicuous. You don't want to be outshone by your clothes! It is wise to leave bags and other such accessories outside the audition area – they will only get in the way. David sums this up succinctly: 'Take yourself but leave your props at home.'

He goes on to point out the importance of sitting well at an interview. Positioning yourself so your features can be easily seen, facing the interviewer in a way that is attentive, without being forced and strained. Many actors, probably through nerves, avert their eyes, drop their heads or mask their faces with their hands or their hair. This makes it difficult for the interviewer to communicate with them or to gauge their possible impact on an audience. He also warns against smoking: nowadays, when so many people have given it up, it can antagonise. Another important comment he makes is about the focus and delivery of an audition speech. 'Don't act the speech at the director.' He explains that this can be both embarrassing and distracting. It infers that the director is expected to react in some way, which in the context of an audition is inappropriate. The director is trying to remain objective in order to assess your talent and suitability for the part; forcing a director to become part of the performance will only alienate him or her.

Most on the receiving end of such speeches would heartily concur with this, but there are a few instances when it would not apply. If you are performing a prologue, an epilogue or where it is clear the playwright intends you to address the audience, it is quite acceptable for you to include the viewer or viewers as one of their number without 'eyeballing' them.

David finishes by stressing how competitive the fringe has become. He urges actors to prepare for auditions with as much care and preparation as if it were for any West End production – the competition will be as great and the audition process can be as stringent.

## Alison Chard, casting director, Royal Shakespeare Company

Alison Chard lists what she considers to be five essential steps for drama students before and after they leave college.

1. Train at an accredited drama school.
2. Actively look for an agent during your final year at drama school.
3. Put a photo in *Spotlight*.
4. Write to every repertory and fringe theatre.
5. If you get a part and succeed in a show, invite as many casting directors as possible. If not, think about setting up your own fringe company with friends.

Putting a photo in *Spotlight* is straightforward enough, involving as it does simply sending off for a form, filling it in and returning it with the appropriate money; finding an agent can prove more difficult. It is important to invite them to see your performances during your final year at drama school. If, however, you find you have graduated without securing one, don't despair. There are actors' co-operatives where the actors club together and work as their own agents – these can be excellent. You can in fact, manage without an agent for a time, certainly when you are first starting out, acting upon Alison's fourth and fifth steps of advice, and asking agents to view you when giving a performance you are pleased with. To be honest it is difficult to gain access to TV and film interviews without representation, since agents have all the necessary contacts. Difficult, but not impossible.

## Audrey Help, assistant to Alison Chard

Audrey Help augmented this with a quote from *Hamlet*, 'To thine own self be true'. A sentiment which would be of use to any actor especially when the struggle for recognition gets tough.

## Maureen Vincent, agent, Peters, Fraser and Dunlop

The agents we approached were mainly concerned with practical matters such as suitable photographs, punctuality and appearance. They all stressed the importance of dressing appropriately for an interview. Maureen Vincent of Peters, Fraser and Dunlop suggested that as a rough guide 'You should dress up for a TV or film interview whereas you can afford to be more casual when going for a theatre job'. This does seem to be the case. TV and film casting directors stressed the fact that wearing a suitable outfit can often influence a director or producer in your favour while theatre directors seem less concerned with dress unless it is intrusive.

## Suzanne Jarrott, Hollywood agent

Suzanne Jarrott, of the Chasin Agency, makes the following comment about the importance of having realistic photos.

> Have good photographs that look like the artist. Producers and directors get very upset to find Danny de Vito standing in front of them, when they are looking at a photograph of Tom Cruise!

This is an important point. It is very tempting to choose the photographs that are most flattering but remember you are an actor not a model. You may not know exactly what they are looking for but those in the business of casting are likely to be more interested in a face that shows individuality and character rather than posed beauty.

## Matthew Robinson, TV Producer

Matthew Robinson, the well respected and extremely successful TV producer, (both *Byker Grove* and *EastEnders* received accolades and increased ratings under his guardianship), has comprehensive and precise advice for actors auditioning for TV parts:

> First visual impressions count hugely – unfair though that may be. And most directors have an imagination that fails them at auditions so the three 'Golden Do's' when meeting a director new to you are 'Research, Research, Research'. Make your agent find out about the character's age, occupation, temperament, etc. If possible add to your information by ringing the production company. Then put that knowledge to good use. Subtly dress for the part: suit, jeans, brogues, trousers, boots, scarves, hats, glasses, hair (slicked down, centre-parted, bunches, back-combed), make-up (tarty, classy, nun), props (bag, stick, watch-chain). Even if it's period, find a way to allude to the appropriate look.
>
> Also research the director's track record. Then manage to drop in a couple of their past shows – how much you loved it, all the wonderful performances. Be quite shameless. Remember Disraeli on flattery: 'When it comes to royalty, lay it on with a trowel.' Be confident that directors are as susceptible as Queen Victoria. But get your facts right.
>
> One 'Golden Don't': unless you're 99% certain an acquired accent is perfect, go to the ends of the earth to avoid trying one out at auditions. Otherwise you're 99% sure to lose the job. By the way, if the director you're meeting isn't new to you, i.e. you've worked with them before, the audition is likely to be a waste of time. You won't get the job.

## Charles Jarrott, film and TV director

The film and TV director Charles Jarrott, made some astute observations regarding interview behaviour. He has worked for many years on both feature films and TV films. Although he has been based in the States for the past ten years his work continues to command respect on both sides of the Atlantic. His comments are witty but pertinent.

1. In this world of blue jeans and sweatshirts, not a lot of thought goes into how to dress for interviews. Dressing for the part is not a bad idea. If you're up for a doctor or a lawyer, for example, dressing like Marlon Brando in *The Wild One* may not be the way to go. American producers have a tendency to cast the person who fits their mind's eye. The fact that an artist can act and be made to look right by the wardrobe department doesn't always come to their minds.

2. Quell the idea that coming into an interview full of the joys of spring, and cracking with the jokes, will warm the interviewers' hearts. They may have been at it for some long unrewarding time and only want the artist to get on with it in a professional way.

3. Don't be late for an interview. You may have to wait a long time before you're seen but better the error be on the side of the producing company.

## Waris Hussein, TV and film director

Waris Hussein is another director who is equally in demand both in the United States and in the United Kingdom. He has been responsible for many a critically acclaimed 'Movie of the Week'. Recently he has extended his interests even further, developing film projects in Europe and India. He warns that trying to control nerves by assuming an air of false confidence can result in antagonising rather than impressing the interviewer. 'Make yourself accessible without arrogance. A sense of self is not rudeness or pretended indifference.'

He also cautions against over familiarity. He feels that however well you may know the director, casting director, or anyone else who may be present at the interivew, it is a mistake to presume on the friendship, enter into a personal conversation or greet them over effusively in this context.

He also emphasises the need for preparation – find out as much as possible about the director and the script as well as the part. He cites the case of an actor whose first remark on meeting the director was, 'Oh I'm sorry I didn't catch your name'. He didn't get the part! The actor was, in all probability, attempting to give the impression that he was too busy or laid back to bother to learn the director's name, rather than a genuine 'ignorance'. Either way, it's not an approach to be recommended.

## Jill Pearce, film and commercials casting director

Jill Pearce works in the United Kingdom and internationally. She casts both films and commercials and is the United Kingdom's leading casting director for commercials. Such is her expertise, clients are prepared to pay for her to fly all over the world in search of just the right face and personality for the part.

She cautions actors to be prepared to find commercial castings very, very competitive. She points out that so many actors want to appear in them, not only because the money is so good but also because they get to work with some of the world's best directors (clients can pay to get virtually who they want), and they often get to travel, all expenses paid.

She feels that acting in commercials calls for a special technique. Everything is very immediate. Actors have to be extremely clever and have enough skill to be able to arrive at a performance within a moment. Many experienced theatre actors fail because they take too long to reach performance level. There is no time to build a character, you must be the person instantly. The use of eyes is of paramount importance. 'The eyes are actually the whole story' was how Jill put it.

Dress is also very important. Turn up in clothes that are suitable for the role. For example, don't arrive in jeans and a sloppy sweater for the part of an executive, conversely a lounge suit would hardly be right for a farmer. Casting directors give precise details on the character when arranging the interview, so make sure they are passed on to you and that you act upon them.

'Skill and appearance' is how Jill summed up what she considers to be the most salient factors when casting commercials. Like so many casting directors she feels that her job is 'friendly mediator', in this instance standing between client and artist, appreciating both points of view, supporting and serving their separate needs but finally bringing them together in order to make a successful product.

### Chris Sandford, actor and voice-over artist

Actor Chris Sandford, who is also one of the most successful voice-over artists around, urges that when trying to break into the competitive world of voice-overs 'Remember, you must make a really great show-reel'.

### Janey Gordon, Senior Lecturer in Radio, Luton University

Janey Gordon also has advice concerning the all important show-reel but in this instance it is intended to gain you work as a radio presenter. 'Remember you are selling 'you' in this instance, not the music, so the tape should start off with you introducing a disc or handling a phone-in, rather than your favourite track. Fill those 3–5 minutes with you at your best, demonstrating why they should employ you, rather than anyone else.'

## Angie Brown, actress/partner of Michael Brown Associates

Angie Brown's company Michael Brown Associates specialises in sourcing and casting professional actors for role-play and training in the business field, a comparatively new and useful area of employment for actors but she warns: 'Not every actor will make a good role-player. It's not just a case of creating a character and playing it. Using the brief as a guide, the actor has to constantly adjust his performance, allowing the assessors or trainers to see the candidate demonstrating whatever areas of competence they require for the exercise. They must also give every candidate a fair and equal chance to fully show these strengths and weaknesses. Above all, it's about taking it seriously. Role-play might just be a fill-in job from the actor's point of view, but to the candidate, it is about their career, their future and their life.'

## Sarah Cameron, agent for presenters

The job of 'Presenting' was once filled mainly by journalists but has now become an increasingly popular option for actors. Sarah Cameron from the presenter's agency Take Three Management, has two pieces of valuable advice which could apply equally well to an acting as well as a presenting casting session. The first applies to when you are actually at the casting meeting: 'Although it is very difficult, do try and be as relaxed as possible.' The second is for afterwards: 'If you don't get the job, don't get disheartened and give up trying. Everyone has different tastes – if you didn't get this job you may well get the next one.'

## Serena Hill, casting director, Royal National Theatre

Serena Hill, the vital young casting director for the Royal National Theatre, is another who liaises between actor and director. She is all too aware how vulnerable actors can be. 'After all', she says, 'they are in the business of talent.' She does, however, have some words of advice and warning. 'Be punctual and prepare properly. Listen to the questions and answer what is being asked.' She goes on to elaborate on this last remark further. 'A great many actors when asked the usual opening question about their recent experience proceed to launch into a lengthy description of the plot of the TV or play they have been working on. Sometimes they even fail to mention the name of the character they played or its place in the storyline. All that is called for is a brief explanation of their character and any aspects of the plot which are relevant to their performance.'

She also comments on how many actors seem to have difficulty in making an exit. 'They seem unwilling to leave, when the interview is clearly at an end.' She suggests that they should try to be sensitive to the mood of the director to realise when they have finished. Then get up, say goodbye and leave the room as quickly as possible. She hastily added that she didn't mean, suddenly spring to your feet and rush for the door, but simply to go as briskly and gracefully as possible. To make this easier put on your coat after you have left the room and keep bags, etc. to a minimum.

The business of leaving at the end of the interview can be tricky. Nerves sometimes make even the most agile of us clumsy and the most simple action like rising from a chair and picking up your belongings can become fraught with difficulty. If you feel this could be the case, although it might sound ridiculous, it's worth practising the routine once or twice before you leave for the interview, just to give yourself confidence. Knowing when to leave is easier when you learn to recognise the signs. Some directors make it abundantly clear with a kindly but dismissive phrase or nod. Others use a more subtle approach, such as looking down and going through their papers, or turning to speak to someone else. As a rough guide, when they shift their attention from you it's a signal to leave. If you should get it wrong they will always stop you – a preferable option to sitting or standing uncertain whether to move.

Selina ended by saying that she felt that her job as casting director was to 'try and make the time the actor spent with the director as valuable as possible.' This is a sentiment shared by all the casting directors I spoke to. They are aware of how important an interview is to an actor and how nerves can make the experience into an ordeal.

## Sweetpea Slight, assistant to Thelma Holt

Sweetpea Slight is another talented young woman connected with casting. Not strictly a casting director, she is Thelma Holt's assistant and in that capacity is closely involved with the casting process of their many distinguished and successful productions. She is with the production from its conception, working with Thelma, so that the casting of every part from the lead to the smallest role, becomes an integral part of the process of production.

Sweetpea shares with Serena Hill a respect for an actor's talent: she understands and appreciates the pressure they are under at auditions but warns them to be careful lest nerves should manifest themselves as arrogance, rudeness or limit answers to monosyllabic replies. She reminds them that casting is a two-way process. The person casting can be as nervous of making the wrong decision and choosing the wrong artiste as the actor is of not getting the part.

Sweetpea feels, like many others involved in the casting process, that an interview is sufficient to show an actor's talent and potential. She says she can tell almost immediately who is likely to get the part, although she admits it is difficult to define why. 'A sense of something unknown and exciting waiting to be released,' is how she puts it.

## Herbie Wise, TV director

Herbie Wise is a director who is respected throughout the profession. Renowned for his empathy with actors as well as the quality of his work, his experience spans many years. His successes range from the fabled series *I, Claudius* to the more recent *Brother Cadfael*.

Herbie is unusual in that he has never asked an actor to read for a part. He says he can tell all he needs to know from their personality and conversation. Many others agree with this in theory but few dare to put it into practice. He declares he has only made one or two mistakes over the years. He does, however, sometimes turn the tables on the actor and ask them to interview *him*. He likes actors to be lucid and intelligent, 'to have views on things' to use his words. He also wants them to be honest about themselves. This last, he realises, has to be treated with discretion. He admits that many directors need strong indications that the actor is exactly right for the part. If they are casting a housewife they want to see a housewife. The smart actor assesses the character of the director and adjusts his approach accordingly.

## Nigel Hawthorne, actor and director

Nigel Hawthorne also advocates a simple and direct manner at an interview. 'Just because you are an actor don't act.' However, Nigel is an actor of international repute and many years experience, who has recently added directing successfully to his accomplishments. He therefore brings to the job both at rehearsals and in the casting process all his considerable knowledge of acting. He understands that the craft entails taking on a personality and circumstances that are not your own. Unfortunately, most directors don't trust this phenomenon. They need proof and reassurance when they are interviewing. This is borne out by the casting director, Doreen Jones.

## Doreen Jones, casting director

Doreen is one of the United Kingdom's leading casting directors. Internationally respected, she has been responsible for casting such prestigious series as *Brideshead Revisited* and *Prime Suspect*. She rarely asks an actor to read for her during an interview – with her years of experience, skill as an interviewer plus her own special gift for spotting talent, she finds it unnecessary. She warns, however, that when an actor is called in to meet a director for a specific role, they should not only be prepared to read if asked, but also do as much background preparation for the part as possible. Research the environment, read any books that provide relevant information, explore similar social conditions to that of the character and any particular traits or circumstances that are peculiar to them. This way you are able to relate more fully to the part and also show a passion for your job as an actor.

Appearance and clothes are also important. Not to the extent of coming virtually in costume but a commonsense approach, indicating that you could believably play the part. She cites a case of what not to do. When she was casting a series, which is set in 1930, a young actor was called in to be considered for the part of a young aristocrat. He arrived with designer stubble and jeans.

She suggests that actors should feel that they can contribute more to the conversation at an interview. For example, when asked what parts they have played lately, instead of just stating the name, it would be much more effective and useful if they would give an outline of the types of characters they played and their journeys through the plots, and to elaborate on a role that is similar to the present one. In fact, if the actor themself has undergone an experience or has a background that is relevant they should mention it. If the part is in an accent that is different from your own, be sure that you give some indication that you can do it, by telling a story or anecdote that involves your using the accent. In fact anything that shows that you have an understanding or an affinity with the role should be brought into the conversation.

Doreen makes another important point. The actor should realise that they can ask to read again if they feel that their first effort could be improved on. She even goes as far as to say that it would be wise always to request it. The second time, nerves are more under control and the focus and purpose of the scene is clearer in the mind. She confesses that she often longs to suggest it but hesitates to intervene between the actor and director at this stage.

She has some valuable advice for young actors who have just left drama school. First of all for those who have received little or no training in television technique (a week or two on a college production is not enough), find out where any films or TV films are being shot on location, and go and watch as unobtrusively as possible. Spend time, (being sure to keep well out of the artiste's sight lines), studying what is being required of the actors, their use of props, marks, lighting, continuity, etc. Try to learn the terminology. This way, when you land your first TV job, you will have more of an idea of what will be expected of you.

Her next point concerns the use of the weekly casting publications. Only answer specific ads, and when you do send off your details bear in mind that the photo need only be postcard size, or, if you are in *Spotlight*, just a photocopy of a photo for quick reference is all that is necessary.

Next, while she appreciates the opportunities that fringe gives to the young to display their talents, she urges actors to make sure they are satisfied that the role and their performance of it does them justice, before they ask casting directors to view it.

Finally, she advocates continuing classes once you have left drama school. This is something that actors in the United States take very seriously but in the United

Kingdom actors are more reluctant to take advantage of the courses and teachers that are available. Such classes are well worth pursuing – they keep your skills honed and show that you still have an enthusiasm for your work.

One feels that Doreen has a passionate admiration for acting talent, and a special sensitivity towards actors and their problems. In an interview, she will not only mediate between them and the director, but also provide them with a protective shield of support. However, she does urge actors to sustain their enthusiasm and dedication to their craft despite the inevitable disappointments, and suggests that they let this be apparent in the way they prepare and research for the particular role for which they are being considered. An ideal example of this is Peter Capaldi, a well-established actor, who not only agreed to attend an interview and read for the part of the transsexual in *Prime Suspect* but went out of his way to research the part. He met and studied transsexuals, read books on the subject and even went so far as to discover an elocution teacher who specialised in helping them adapt their voices to make them more believably female. He was thus able to reproduce accurately the breathy delivery that most transsexuals assume – he got the job!

### Paul Annett, TV and film director

Someone else who responds favourably to enthusiasm in an actor is Paul Annett. Paul has directed on both sides of the Atlantic but is perhaps best known for his work on such well-loved series as *Poldark*, *The Secret Army*, *Sherlock Holmes* and, more recently, *EastEnders*, where he both directs and produces the 'specials'.

Paul suggests that it is important for actors to be enthusiastic not only about their own work but also about the job in question when they come for an interview. In his experience, some actors, perhaps through nerves or a mistaken notion that it might impress, take it upon themselves to criticise the script or point out what they consider to be wrong with the particular series. Besides being tactless it is also unnecessary. The director is usually only too aware of any faults and the last thing they need is an actor to point them out. They realise that miracles can be, and frequently are, wrought by an actor with zeal and talent. Many indifferent scripts have received glowing critical acclaim due to this phenomenon. Also, as Paul observes, 'you are hardly going to cast anyone who obviously despises the project, whereas you will be warmly disposed towards the actor who appears interested and excited at the possibility of working on the part. Remember, the director is human and just as vulnerable to insecurities as the actor.'

## Terry Hands, Director Emeritis, Royal Shakespeare Company

Terry Hands offers valuable advice to actors on the choice and presentation of audition speeches. He has found these to be, for him, the most effective way of spotting talent, although he does qualify this by pointing out that the requirements of the RSC are somewhat different than those of the 'one-off' play.

He suggests that speeches that are intended to be performed as monologues, such as soliloquies, prologues and epilogues, often make the most successful audition speeches. They give the actor the opportunity to play to the auditioner and to use their own personality, qualities that Terry considers important. He urges actors to be sure they know the speeches very, very well. Auditions are inevitably a nerve-racking occasion but if you are really certain of your piece, it will relieve the pressure considerably. He, like so many of those who are in the business of casting, wants to reassure actors that those who are holding the auditions are usually all too aware of how the actors are feeling. Most are sympathetic and anxious to put them at their ease as much as possible; in reality, they are often nervous themselves. After all, the onus is on them to make the right decision.

This may be difficult to credit when your knees are shaking and your teeth chattering but so many directors have made the same remark that it clearly must be the case. It certainly will make them seem a little less formidable when you find yourself in the position of trying to convince them you are 'right for the part'.

## Thelma Holt, theatre producer

Thelma Holt is renowned as an innovative and courageous producer. She has worked alongside many of the world's finest theatre directors and her contribution to the theatre is equal to any; however, the fact that she has also been an actress makes her advice particularly informed. She has viewed the scene from both sides. Her contribution is succinct but with far reaching implications. 'Remember you have a choice. You don't have to accept the job.' She feels that too often actors forget this fact. They are so anxious to acquit themselves well at the interview or audition that they ignore the possibility that, if they are 'right' for the part, those casting will be just as anxious that the actor accept the part as the actor is to receive an offer.

If you can absorb this concept and let it affect your approach to an interview it will add greatly to your self-esteem and confidence. You will then see yourself in the position of considering a part rather than just waiting to be chosen – you will be playing an active not a passive role.

Reading through all the comments and the advice given, one fact will have become clear to you – how similar they are. There are a few personal foibles and preferences but for the most part, whatever their particular input to the casting process might be, those asked come up with the same observations and advice again and again, albeit in different guises. Paramount was preparation – not only of the script but of yourself. When you go to an audition you must know the speeches backwards but also have enough knowledge of the proceedings to deal with any eventuality – not to mention cope with the whim and mood of the director.

At all castings the ability to sight-read well is imperative if you are to do yourself and your talent justice; the skill must be second nature to you. You need to have a clear idea of the purpose and structure of interviews and casting sessions, an idea of the possible pitfalls and how to avoid them as well as what will be expected of you, in order to give of your best. Unfortunately drama schools and colleges, however excellent in other ways, rarely provide students with sufficient training in these areas. Few teach sight-reading or interview technique, and while some allot a period for work on audition speeches, this invariably turns out to be just enough time to find out what you are doing wrong but not enough to explore fully the possibilities of how to choose material wisely and then to put it across effectively.

Happily there are ways of working on these things for yourself once you have left college, or during the vacations if you are still studying. The following chapters will provide you with all the relevant information and techniques that you will need in order to prepare yourself for casting sessions in all branches of the media: warnings of the problems you might encounter and advice on how to avoid them; step-by-step instructions on how to improve your sight-reading; guidance on choosing and working on audition speeches and coping with the interview; plus a run down of the methods used to cast everything from fringe to film.

# 2

# *The Audition*

What does the term 'audition' mean nowadays? It used
to refer to occasions when actors were given the opportunity to demonstrate their talent before potential
employers. They would perform one or more prepared
speeches in front of a director or selection panel who
would then decide whether or not to engage them. With
the advent of films, TV and other branches of the media
from which an actor can get work, this has changed.
The method of selecting actors has diversified and
modified to suit the various requirements of each particular form of employment. These all come under the
general heading of 'Casting'. An audition has come to
mean a specific way in which an actor is given a chance
to display their skill in order to be cast or chosen, and it
is used mainly for hiring actors for work in the theatre
or picking applicants for a drama course at a school or
college. This is not to infer that it is no longer so important for you to be able to perform an audition speech
well, the skill is vital to any actor, but simply to point
out that the audition is now only one aspect of the
casting system.

Choosing the speeches and working on them can be a
daunting task but with guidance can become exciting
and stimulating.

## The audition speech

**1. Choosing your material** At an audition your choice of material already says a lot about you. It says whether or not you have taken the trouble to explore beyond the beaten path and whether your dramatic sense has helped you choose material that is appropriate to your age and abilities. In other words, cast yourself intelligently. Find a role you could actually play – one that is near to your own age and that doesn't involve your assuming an unfamiliar accent, a funny walk or voice or any other applied mannerism that might detract from your performance. There are plenty of books containing audition material on the market – and we make some suggestions for audition speeches in Chapter 7 – but it's also worth looking at radio plays, film scripts, television plays* and even novels.

Here are some points to consider when you are making the search.

**2. Length of speech** Keep it short, about two and a half minutes is the usual requirement and that's about right. You can get across a lot in that time. People all too often think there's something virtuous in wandering on for five minutes and in so doing they run the risk of irritating the auditioner and/or being stopped. In fact most of those involved with casting from audition speeches admit that they make up their minds after the first thirty seconds, so if you fall in love with a speech that only lasts a minute and a half and you feel it really shows off your talent, it would be quite acceptable.

**3. What to avoid** Best avoided are the Hamlets, the Ophelias, the Violas and the Lady Macbeths. Your panel or director will frequently have pronounced views

---

*These can be found at any theatrical bookshop, such as Samuel French or Offstage in Chalk Farm, London. Alternatively, the big chain bookshops such as Waterstones usually stock some of the better known radio and television plays.

on how these characters need to be played and will be less than forgiving if you should drop even a syllable.

Also best avoided is the speech which forms a climax in the play. You will not have had the narrative impetus to help you reach this point nor will the listeners. Ophelia's mad scene is a good example of this; an atrociously difficult speech even within the context of a production but without its narrative setting the audience has not had a chance to catch up emotionally with the character, and the actress is obliged to travel to a state of extreme emotional turmoil in less than a second. The result is usually fey and generalised. Generalised emotion is the last thing you want to convey at your audition.

It is sensible to avoid a speech which includes another character speaking, dialogue in other words. Asking a fellow auditionee to read in for you is much too chancy an operation and to play your lines omitting the others will be disjointed and difficult for the listeners to follow and almost impossible for you to play.

Props are best avoided. If they are absolutely essential and you can't manage without them they should be chosen very carefully and their handling taken fully into account. For example, the letter in Julia's speech in *Two Gentlemen of Verona*. You must remember to clear props up afterwards; this needs to be planned and rehearsed as part of your departure from the room or stage to save yourself embarrassment on the day.

In fact a safe rule to follow is: if a prop is easy to handle and unobtrusive it should be all right, but if it needs managing, then it's best forgotten.

For instance, a panel of auditioners was once obliged to grind its teeth with impatience, while a girl set out a four piece tea-service. Not a good idea. It is unwise to build your speech around a specific piece of furniture. The most you can reasonably expect at an audition is a chair. Even then it's not going to be the same as the one you rehearsed with, and it could easily end up being just another thing with which to cope.

Be wary of choosing a speech with an accent that you are not completely at home with, even if it appears ideal in every other way. If the accent is unbelievable it will only detract from your performance and if you feel uncertain about it this will add an unnecessary tension to the occasion.

**4. What to look for** Look for a speech that shows off as many facets of the character as possible, one that contains plenty of thought changes and isn't on one emotional note. An effective audition speech has a strong emotional journey but also a sense of argument reaching some sort of resolution by the end of it. This doesn't mean that it has to end in a decision but that it doesn't simply trail off. A speech that tells a story often offers excellent opportunities but make sure that as the narrator you have a strong emotional involvement in it. Remember the object of the speech is to show off your abilities: the more variations of emotion and thought you can show, the more successfully this will be achieved.

Most people are aware that they should choose contrasting speeches. However, they often limit this consideration to that of period and the categories of tragedy and comedy. But it is also important to bear in mind contrasts in style, content, the character's personality and environment and the physical requirements of the speech.

A word about the categories of period. Most companies or drama colleges stipulate one modern and one classical speech but few define the terms further. 'Classical' usually refers to plays written in the Elizabethan period (this obviously includes Shakespeare) and Jacobean period and could encompass foreign playwrights such as Molière, Racine, Marivaux etc. But the Restoration period and plays by Shaw, Chekhov, Wilde and those written at the turn of the century are more borderline, so check that they are acceptable before using them in this category. The term 'modern' covers any play written during and since the 1960s. Don't agonise too long over the choice of piece. If you keep in mind the do's and don'ts listed, find a speech that you like and a character you can relate to, you can't go far wrong. In the final analysis although the choice of speech is important, it is the way you work on it that matters most.

### Working on the speech

Having settled on your choice of speech or speeches it is now time for the 'nitty gritty' of getting down to work on them.

1. Read the play from which the speech has been taken (if it's a monologue specifically written for audition purposes, that will be dealt with later). It is virtually impossible to get the best from the speech if you cannot place it in its context. Also, you may have to field questions on the play from the people auditioning you.

2. Don't immediately learn it off by heart. This is a disastrous way to learn a speech. If you learn it off parrot fashion this is how it will stick in your mind and should you ever 'dry' (forget your lines) in performance, panic is likely to make you refer to this birdlike recitation because that is how you first absorbed them. The best way to learn lines is to assimilate them. That is, almost by osmosis, as you work on the thoughts, emotions and physical responses of the text, so that each word and phrase is linked to the character's physical and emotional state at that particular moment. This way, not only are you less likely to dry but should you do so (and it happens to most actors at one time or another), you will at least know what your character is feeling and can ad lib more readily until the line comes back to you.

3. Remember there is no such thing as a speech. We don't plan to speak for a long period of time, it just

happens that for a number of reasons we go on talking. One thought leads us on to another, we get carried away by our enthusiasm for developing an idea, we are trying to provoke a response from the person we are addressing and if they don't reply we continue our verbal prodding, or we are endeavouring to resolve an argument, etc., etc. The important point for you as an actor is the realisation that this outburst of verbalised feeling and thoughts is extempore, it hasn't been planned. You are speaking because you have just thought of something you want to say.

4. Start with yourself. You are the character. Don't fall into the trap of judging them in any way. You don't like or dislike them, they are you. You have to see the world through their eyes.

5. Read over the speech several times before you begin working on it in detail. Don't make decisions too early. If you have time, it is a good idea to read it over several times then leave it for a day. When you come back to it you will have digested all the initial information and you will be surprised at how much more you will discover when you approach it with fresh eyes.

6. Ask the four 'W' questions, i.e.:
   - What has happened before the speech begins?
   - What are you doing?
   - Who are you talking to? (Remember if the answer to this one is the audience you still have a relationship with them.)
   - What do you need?

Let's deal with each question in greater detail and explore why they will be of value to you.

*What has happened before the speech begins?* As has been said, it is very important to read the play from which the speech has been taken. If for some reason this is not possible, make up a believable context for it yourself. In order to find out the character's motives and needs, you have to find out as much as you can about their background, environment, lifestyle and outlook on life from the text or, failing that, your imagination. It is also vital to know what has occurred immediately before the speech starts so that you have an insight into the character's state of mind, the thoughts and feelings from which the speech springs.

*What are you doing?* In other words, what is the underlying action of the speech, i.e. I argue, I tease, I persuade, etc. This provides you with a strong verb to play with, giving purpose and energy to the speech.

*Who are you talking to?* This is straightforward enough but remember that the answer must include your emotional relationship with that person. Because at an audition they will be there only in your imagination you must be sure that you establish them and your attitude to them very clearly both before you start the speech and throughout it.

*What do you want?* In order to answer this you have to decide why you are speaking. We never speak without reason. We want a response or reaction in return. Even if we are speaking to ourselves it is for some reason. In answering this question you find the character's motivation for the speech.

Having decided on your answers make sure you communicate your findings through the speech. Knowing is not enough – sharing your knowledge with your audience is what matters.

The chapter on sight-reading also covers these questions. The advice is slightly different for sight-reading since you have less time in which to prepare.

If you are working on a monologue that has been written solely for use as audition material, you will have to do a bit of extra work. Your imagination will have to provide you with a background, a context and a recipient of the dialogue in which you can believe, in order to give yourself a foundation of circumstance to work from and a focus for the speech. In other words, if you have no text from which to obtain the answers to the 'W' questions, you have to make up a scenario in which to place your character.

7. Be careful not to impose a generalised emotional label on the speech, such as 'he is angry' or 'she is upset'. Try to deal in moments. Our emotions change from minute to minute in subtle ways; play the moment.

8. Don't make up your mind too quickly about the speech. Let ideas suggest themselves as you work on it. Keep an open mind and the speech will yield more information.

9. Look for the key words, the changes in emotion and thought, and the climatic points. Be greedy for things to play. The more aspects of the character you find to play, the more 'things are going on' in the speech, the more secure you will feel and, surprisingly maybe, the easier it will be to play. (This refers to internal and emotional work rather than any applied extraneous mannerisms or physicality.)

10. Don't plan a lot of supposedly impressive or showy moves before you have really studied the speech. Let them evolve slowly as you work on it so they arise naturally out of the needs of the character and in response to the text. Remember that we never move without a reason even if we are unconscious of it: each move must tell us more about the character and their circumstances and can give valuable clues to the feelings underlying the speech or enforce what is being said.

Of course there are practical considerations to be taken into account. The auditioner needs to see you, especially your face, so don't spend most of your time looking upstage or with your back to them. While it is good to make full use of the playing area, you can't be sure of its size until you get to the audition, so bear this in mind and adapt your moves accordingly when you see the space available. As a general rule, drama schools and repertory companies provide you with a large playing area but at an audition for a fringe theatre you can end up acting on the proverbial postage stamp.

When you make a move, *really* make it. Whether it is a hand gesture, a step or a walk, do it wholeheartedly, make it definite. If you only half do it or look as if you aren't sure, this will detract from what you are saying. Every move must have focus and meaning. Similarly, be careful not to adopt affected attitudes – a character's physicality is an essential part of their personality and everything they feel will affect their body in some way, however subtly.

11. Remember, volume is not emotion. This is an important point as all too often actors confuse intensity of emotion with extremes of volume, and either shout or whisper under the mistaken impression that they convey deep feeling. The first is impossible to listen to for any but the shortest period of time: the noise obliterates the text, the listener is unable to take in any nuances of meaning, the sound overwhelms everything else that is happening. This can make your audience feel under attack and alienated. Whispering is inaudible, leaving the audience irritated rather than moved.

12. Observe punctuation. It is the playwright's means of giving you clues as to the character's thought and emotional changes. 'Put plenty of air around full stops'; that is, give yourself time to really play the changes of gear, find the extension of the thought or the new idea. Commas, semicolons and colons are also changes but on a smaller scale – these can be a subtle difference in the level of emotional energy, a moment's hesitation in the flow of thought or a slight change of direction in the line of argument. Ask yourself why they are there and use them to help you find out more about the character and the author's intentions.

## Beginnings and endings

First of all, remember that, strictly speaking, beginnings and endings are not beginnings and endings. Your character is not making a beginning, the speech is just a part of their life. When you are working on a speech it is a good idea to work in a few moments of thought to lead you into the actual text. This way your first line will be in response to some stimulus rather than a statement arising from thin air. Make sure you clearly establish your state of mind and your relationship to the recipient of your speech before you start.

Similarly with endings, the character, unless they're drawing their last breath, goes on living and thinking after the end of the speech. Work out what they will be thinking after they finish speaking, then play that thought at the end of the speech before reverting to yourself. Don't impose a false ending by trying to bring things artificially to a conclusion. This doesn't mean stopping abruptly or leaving a thought in mid-air but simply finding a reason to stop speaking at a point that arises convincingly from the text.

## Presenting the speech

1. First and foremost, the most important factor of all – remember that you are in the business of communication. Your purpose and responsibility are to reach people with the playwright's ideas. You are the instrument through which their talents are communicated to an audience. Bear this in mind when rehearsing and presenting your speech. It is important for you to relate to the character, to know as much as possible as to what is going on in the speech, what the author's intentions are and then to convey all you have discovered through your talent to the audience. Make sure you are audible and visible. Beware of self indulgence: if you are feeling the emotions deeply, be certain that the onlookers are also involved and moved. Build carefully to every

climax in the piece, ensuring that you are making all the important points clear along the way.

2. Your physical position when you give the speech is important. Gauge the right distance between you and the viewers. Too near is off-putting and intimidating for you and them. Too far is giving you and them unnecessary difficulties as far as audibility and subtlety of playing are concerned. Of course it will depend on the playing area, but in a largish space about twelve to fifteen feet away is a good distance. In a small space get as far back as you can, allowing for any moves you have that take you upstage. You don't want to end up pressed against the back wall.

3. Remember you are being judged as soon as you enter the room. If you are nervous, announcing yourself and giving the titles of your speeches in a clear and composed way can be more difficult than it sounds. It is a good idea to rehearse your introductions at the same time as the speeches a few times so the introductions become an integral part of the performance.

4. Don't lumber yourself with coats, bags, etc. in the audition room – leave them outside.

5. You don't need to give copies of your speeches to the auditioners. They are not going to prompt you, and while you are performing they want to watch you, not follow the text.

6. Take time to focus your attention before you start each speech. Establish for yourself and your audience who you are speaking to, where they are and your relationship to them. Once this is done you only need to glance at them when necessary during the speech. It can be difficult to set the height of an imaginary person; if you are not careful, they end up getting taller and taller as the speech progresses. If your speech involves another character rather than addressing the audience or a soliloquy, rehearse a few times with someone standing

in for them – this will make it easier to get used to focusing on a constant height.

7. Don't be thrown if the director stops you before you have finished and starts to give you notes or direction. It's usually a good sign, it shows they are interested enough to bother.

8. When you have finished your speeches, smile at the director or panel, say 'Thank you' and leave the room. If they want to talk to you or see anything further they will stop you – but nothing is worse for your morale at that point than standing there awkward and unsure of what to do next.

9. Drying can be traumatic. If you have learned the speech as has been suggested, you are much less likely to dry. However, the unaccountable can occur, something unforeseen can throw your concentration and cause you to dry. Should this happen, don't panic or step out of character, or apologise or ask what you should do. Remain in character, look down, lowering your eyes and breathe out. Remember, the pause that is taking place, which seems to be lasting forever to you, is probably a matter of seconds. Nine times out of ten, bringing the focus of the eyes down releases the tension, clears the brain and the word or phrase will come back to you. If it doesn't and you are totally lost, you will have to come out of character, apologise to the auditioners and request permission to start again. Should they be hard-hearted and refuse, insisting that you pick it up where you left off, take your time to get back into the character, the emotion and the moment. If you continue the speech well all need not be lost. Most directors are sympathetic – after all, they want to know whether you can act, rather than whether you can remember audition speeches.

## Summing up

It is worth while slowly building up a repertoire of speeches. Choose ones along the guidelines given, where you can relate to the character, where your imagination is excited and where there is something strong to play. This will not only provide you with a useful set of pieces but give you a chance to keep acting in between jobs. It is important that they become old friends: work on them until they almost become second nature to you. Keep them topped up, you may be called on to perform them at very short notice. Only start to work on a new one when you feel you could play your present ones easily and confidently in any possible circumstances.

Lastly, and most importantly of all; ENJOY. Enjoy working on them, rehearsing them and, above all, performing them. They are a chance to do what you love – act.

# 3

## *The Interview*

How does one word – interview – conjure up so many conflicting emotions? Excitement and exhilaration at having got one; apprehension at the thought of actually participating in one. There seems so much at stake, often the chance of a job depends on the outcome of one meeting. This can be said to be true of any interview for a job; however, with the actor there are some crucial differences. The ability to handle an interview well has to become a necessary skill; attending interviews regularly is part of an actor's way of life. The nature of the profession is such that the majority of the jobs are temporary and therefore an actor will be chosen afresh for each new engagement; interviewing is an integral part of this selection process. Actors also have to come to terms with the fact that their credentials are probably of secondary importance – they are in the business of selling themselves!

Previous experience, answering questions intelligently, dressing appropriately are all valuable assets. But, ultimately, it's their personality that will clinch the deal. Rejection can be devastating, even seasoned actors find it hard to remain sensibly philosophical and yet, logically speaking, given the amount of competition, it would be virtually impossible to get every job you go up for.

Keeping a sense of self-esteem can prove very difficult

in these circumstances. Even when you are successful it's hard to resist trying to analyse why. Did you say something special that did the trick? If so, what was it? Which of your attributes did they find irresistible? What was it they saw in you? *And most of all* – can you do it again? Was it just a fluke? None of this is conducive to a peaceful frame of mind. So what can be done to rectify this state of affairs? Unfortunately there is no magic formula that guarantees you get every job you go up for. But there are ways of lessening the trauma, helping you take it all 'more in your stride', the most important thing being your *attitude*. While I am making no wild claims, 'your attitude' is the nearest thing you will find to that magic formula. When it comes to choosing between two people who are both equally talented and right for the part any interviewer will tell you that they will opt for the one who has the air of relaxed, quiet confidence. A respect for yourself and your talent inspires reciprocal feelings in others. How to achieve this miraculous confidence then?

Well, it's not easy in such a competitive profession where insecurity is an inevitable by-product of its structure. But there are practical steps which can take you a long way towards attaining it. It's essential to know as much about the process as possible – knowledge brings familiarity which in turn breeds confidence.

## The purpose of the interview

The concept of interviewing rather than just auditioning or reading, arose from the idea that it would make the process of casting fairer and more actor friendly because:

1. The director will be able to assess whether an actor is open and responsive to direction.

2. The director and the actor will be able to judge how compatible they are and whether their feelings about the part and acting generally coincide.

3. By talking to an actor face to face it will be easier to decide whether their personality is suitable for the part. (I know, I know, you're an actor – it's your job to take on another personality. Unfortunately a great many directors don't feel secure enough to trust this precept.)

4. In an interview situation an actor will become more relaxed and, consequently, give a better account of themselves. This is fine in theory but it presupposes that the interviewer has the talent for putting people at their ease. This can indeed be the case but, unhappily, very frequently it's not. There are some casting directors and directors who whether through overwork or some personal foible seem bent on intimidating the actor, making them feel unimportant and unsure. Conversely, there are directors and producers who are inhibited by actors. They want and admire their talent but are uncertain how to deal with what they consider to be unpredictable and volatile creatures.

Then there are directors who feel just as insecure as any actor. Most are freelance and their next job will depend to a large extent on how well this one goes and maybe the script isn't as good as they hoped, or the producer is giving them a hard time or even their personal life is in turmoil. Whatever the reason, they appear to be in greater need of reassurance than the expectant actor sitting before them. Lastly, there are those who exploit their power, keeping the actor waiting unnecessarily, disregarding their presence when they enter the room or showing no interest in what the actor may have to say. All these possibilities have to be faced and dealt with when necessary.

## How to cope with the interviewer

**1. Remember they are human**    It is easy to lose sight of the fact that the person sitting opposite you waving all that apparent power is just another human being. They are only human and suffering from the same fears and doubts that we all do. If they temporarily appear to have forgotten their human fallibility and are being unbearably grand you can always resort to the old trick of imagining them stark naked in embarrassing circumstances. One of the assets of being an actor is having a vivid imagination!

**2. Don't be a victim**   Instead of approaching the interview as if you were a lamb to the slaughter, vaguely hoping that the interviewer will take pity on you and decide to be friendly, go in as if you are genuinely looking forward to meeting those present. Use your actor's antennae to sense their mood, their style and try to tune in a bit. This is not for a moment to suggest that you should ingratiate yourself or take over the interview but rather respond to them as you would if you were a guest in their house. Notice if their greeting is casual or if they use a more formal approach and adjust your manner accordingly. Acknowledge everyone in the room (remembering Waris Hussein's warning not to be over familiar with individuals however well you may know them out of this environment, see pages 17–18) before concentrating more fully on the main interviewers.

**3. Listen to what is being said**   It is so easy to let nerves partially deafen you so you only take in a fraction of what the other person is saying. If you really concentrate, not only is the information you receive valuable, but you will find that your anxiety begins to lessen as your focus changes from yourself to the topic in hand.

**4. Have some answers ready**   Interviewers are not renowned for originality when it comes to questioning, so you can work out a few responses for the most predictable ahead of time. For example, you can pretty well count on being asked the following two questions: 'Why do you think you are right for this part?', 'What have you been up to lately?' This last can be a heartstopper if you haven't worked for some time.

Several casting directors, who for reasons that will become obvious prefer to remain nameless, confided that in this situation it is often better to use creative invention rather than admit shamefacedly to months without work. This may seem an outrageous suggestion but directors are only human and they cannot help but be influenced by your answer. If you haven't worked for a considerable period they may, if they are compassionate creatures, offer you a small part, but they are unlikely to chance giving you a substantial role unless there are exceptional circumstances, i.e. they want to launch an unknown actor in the role or you are so like the character that they feel confident that typecasting will carry the day. One of the main reasons they ask the question is in order to find out the kind of work you have done and the type of characters you have played. Bearing this in mind, one casting director pointed out that this awkward question can even be turned to your advantage. If you say that you have played a role similar to the one that is being cast it can help them see you in the part.

It would be foolhardy of me to endorse this recommendation – apart from its slightly questionable morality, it demands very strong nerves and enough presence of mind to deal with the situation should anyone call your bluff. Having said that, it must be admitted that many actors have done just that and successfully landed plum roles as a result.

If you feel that your circumstances call for desperate measures and decide to chance your luck, bear in mind the following important points: first, make sure that you could have believably played the roles in question, arm yourself with comments on the part and people's reaction to your performance (intelligent observations as to how you could have improved your performance, and what you learned from the experience, not just how good you were!). Choose a venue for the imaginary production that is off the beaten track where there is not the remotest chance your interviewers would have been. Should you prefer to start your life of crime in a smaller way, an imaginary commercial in a foreign country is perhaps a safer bet. If, however, you agree with me and many directors that honesty is the best policy, answer obliquely by telling them about other interesting things you may have been doing while resting, i.e. 'I haven't worked that much recently because I have been busy...' (Painting the house, baby-sitting, temping will not do – starting a business, learning French, moving house, are all possibilities.)

Other questions frequently asked that can be difficult to answer off the cuff are 'How do you see yourself?' or, along similar lines, 'What parts do you like to play?' Both can, in fact, provide you with the opportunity to establish your suitability for the role. Pick out certain experiences or qualities that you find rewarding to play or with which you feel an empathy and that are integral to the part that is being cast. The question 'Where are you from?' can also be used to good effect even if you come from the other side of the world from where the action takes place. Answer in such a way that will enable you to introduce any experience or knowledge that might connect you with the character. For example: 'I grew up in Manchester but reading about life in Detroit I can see great similarities in experience,' etc. In other words in replying to any question use it as a link to carry on the conversation and bring in any information that will demonstrate your ability to relate to the part, or any relevant research you have done in preparation for the interview.

Occasionally the casting director or one of the others present may ask you a question but this is rare. Nevertheless it is important to include everyone when making your replies, regardless of who has initiated the question. Don't forget that you can ask some as well. Interviewers are usually impressed by a question that shows an intelligent interest in the role, the script or the production itself.

Above all, avoid the temptation to be facetious or witty just because you've heard the question a million times before. This will only alienate the interviewers. They expect you to realise that they are not in the business of making clever conversation but in finding the right person for the role.

**5. Don't rely on sex appeal**   Be wary of flirting. Many directors find it irritating or embarrassing or if they do respond things might not work out as you anticipated. You may end up with a date but not necessarily the job.

**6. Be prepared**   Find out as much as you can about the show, the director, the writer and anything else that might be relevant. It will give you something to talk about and no one is above being flattered and pleased if someone has appreciated their past work and can make intelligent references to it. (Only favourable ones. Now is not the time to prove your integrity and share any criticisms you might have with them. Not if you want the job!) Find out as much as you can about the part before you get there, although this can often be difficult. Pressurise your agent for as much detailed information as possible so that you can expose that aspect of your personality which seems most applicable to the part. Bear in mind all that Doreen Jones recommended in Chapter 1. Research in every way that you can, not only the character but also the background and locale of the script. This will impress your interviewers and add greatly to your own confidence. You will feel you have something to contribute to the conversation and be able to point out (or skilfully invent) parallels between you and the role.

**7. Dealing with rudeness and indifference**   It would be nice to say this could never happen or that it would be an unlikely or isolated occurrence – unfortunately that would be misleading and inaccurate. It is better to face it as a possibility and prepare yourself in advance. Here are two of the most common scenarios:

**a.** A casting director has arranged for you to meet a director. You enter the room and greet its occupants. There is a pause, then the casting director returns your greeting, this may be followed by subdued responses from anyone else present. The director sits silent, barely glancing at you. The casting director introduces you and valiantly tries to get a conversation going, but in vain. It is obvious that the director is not interested, in fact, is determinedly not interested. You'll have to cut your losses. Keep cool, there's nothing to be gained by being rude in return. Be utterly charming to the casting director and quit the room as soon as possible. This experience although unpleasant can have a compensatory outcome. The casting director, incensed by the director's behaviour, will usually go out of their way to fix you up with another interview. The director has alienated not only you but them, by ignoring their recommendation in such a high-handed manner.

**b.** The following example is more difficult to cope with. You are sent to meet a casting director who for some reason seems to take a dislike to you on sight. However charming you try to be you fail to impress. This is a tricky situation. Casting directors are very important to actors. While it is unusual for them to give a job outright they have an enormous influence over the director and it is virtually impossible to go up for a TV, movie or commercial, unless they have selected you. For the most part they are the actor's greatest ally in the casting process, their support and championship of new talent has enabled many to get their first break – so this incident needs careful handling. If you challenge them you could make a dangerous enemy, on the other hand, it's obvious you're not going to be their new prodigy. Remain courteous but cool. Don't try to ingratiate yourself, it won't work and you'll only succeed in losing your own self-respect. You may never find out what went wrong. They may well meet you again later and behave as if nothing was amiss or they may never use you. Luckily there are a number of casting directors around and it's unusual not to find one or more who believe in your potential and will take you under their wing.

Both these experiences and those similar are upsetting but remember they have been suffered by most actors. It could even be that you are simply too good-looking. This may sound ridiculous but, especially in the United Kingdom, there is a prejudice that beautiful people can't act. This is totally illogical, especially in a profession where an attractive appearance has proved to be popular with the audience and where there are many examples that disprove the theory. Maybe it's just good old-fashioned jealousy. It can also happen that they have had a personal crisis and they are taking it out on you. Very unfair but very human. But you can bear in mind their human frailty and keep your dignity intact. You will not only survive but be resolved to succeed another day.

There are a couple of other situations that may arise: thankfully these are uncommon.

c. The first is one that people outside the profession presume happens on a regular basis – a director making a pass at an actor. In fact, it is a rare occurrence but awkward to deal with. If their feelings are reciprocated there is obviously no problem; however, if not, the situation requires delicacy. Smiling procrastination followed a few minutes later by the mention of a husband, wife or partner can work quite well but if this appears to have little effect you may have to cut your losses and make a polite but speedy withdrawal. It is sensible to report the incident to your agent as this will protect you from any possible repercussions.

**d.** The second is the curious reaction some directors affect after the actor has finished reading or performing an audition speech. They sit gazing into space in complete silence. The poor actor is uncertain whether their performance was so earth shatteringly dreadful or wonderful that the director is at a loss for words or whether it is an odd form of dismisssal. It is probably wise to smile sweetly and leave, although one actor decided to sit it out and stayed sitting there for about ten minutes after which the director offered him the job, but this seems a chancey option.

If an interview becomes unpleasant for any reason, your best recourse is to leave as quickly and politely as possible. There is nothing to be gained by challenging the offending person or by being rude yourself.

**8. Recognise your own worth** You have something valuable to offer – your talent. You believe you can act otherwise you wouldn't be there, so why shouldn't it be recognised? Without the talent of the actor there would be no show. So often actors feel inferior because they have to wait to be employed in order to practice their craft but then so does the director, the casting director and all the production team. Even the producer is answerable to the backers. And remember what Thelma Holt said – 'You have a choice'. You may want the job but the knowledge that you could turn it down will give you a sense of control over your own destiny.

## What not to do

Remember confidence is not arrogance or aggressive behaviour. Be careful that in an attempt to convince the interviewer of your belief in yourself you don't become opinionated and overbearing. False confidence is just as alienating as false modesty.

**1.** Don't try to impress by assuming an air of affected disinterest, behaving as if you could barely spare the time to attend the interview, answering questions in an offhand manner and implying that you don't care whether you get the job or not. This will ensure that you don't!

2. Alternatively, taking over the interview, asking any number of questions before they can open their mouths, or inferring they will have to prove themselves to you before you will even consider the job, will prove equally unsuccessful.

3. Be wary of trying to be a 'personality'. Being confronted by someone who breaks into peals of laughter or cracks jokes at every given opportunity is irritating and exhausting. On the other hand, the embryo James Dean who sits gazing moodily into the distance and answers any question with a monosyllabic grunt or worse still, the 'Take me as you find me' actor who disagrees on principle with everything that's said or the actor who appears to be making an intentionally provocative statement, i.e. dirty jeans, unbrushed hair, etc., are likely to inspire antagonism rather than respect.

These examples may seem extreme and you may find it difficult to imagine that anyone would behave like that in an interview, but they do happen and not infrequently. Nerves or a misguided notion of how to make an impression can result in the most bizarre conduct.

## What to wear and how to look

If you have read Chapter 1 you will have realised that what you wear and how you look are of some importance. For a start it's one of the first things that will be noticed as you walk into the room. Rightly or wrongly our clothes are seen as an expression of our attitude and personality – so you should wear something that's comfortable and suits you. However, this needs a little elaboration. Comfortable doesn't mean an old sweatshirt, worn-out trainers and a pair of clapped-out jeans, but rather an outfit in which you feel at ease, but look as if you have made a bit of an effort. David Bidmead of the Etcetera Theatre makes an interesting point:

> Be careful of wearing black. Actors of both sexes are apt to wear it as if it were obligatory. Seeing an endless procession of black-clad individuals can make it difficult at the end of a long day's interviewing to remember which is which. The girl in the green dress or the boy in the checked shirt can help distinguish and identify.

On the other hand, don't let your clothes upstage you: fashion victims are remembered for their gear rather than themselves. Then there is the question of dressing the part. As has been said, some directors lack imagination: they need to be reassured that you could look right for the part. This doesn't mean that you have to arrive in full costume but wear something that is in keeping with the period, setting and character. For example, a girl going up for a period drama might wear a longish skirt and a feminine blouse, whereas this outfit would hardly be suitable for the role of a stripper from the Bronx. Similarly with hair and (in the case of girls) make-up. For the most part it is safest to wear your hair in a style that is flattering but not extreme and keep make-up discreet; but if the part calls for something more exaggerated, go with it, bearing in mind the rule about not upstaging yourself.

## Your body language

This does not mean an intense 'Desmond Morris' analysis of your every move but just some common sense observation and hints of how to comport yourself physically during an interview. Remember the purpose of the interview – they want to see you. When you enter the room give a general greeting to everyone present, but make sure to make eye contact with each one individually, however fleetingly, before concentrating your main attention on the principal interviewer. Sit comfortably in your seat but don't lull or sprawl. Rather, lean slightly forward so you appear to be attentive and interested. Face the person addressing you so they can see your features clearly, especially your eyes. This doesn't mean fixing them with a glassy stare, but looking them in the eye naturally as you would normally in conversation. Often there's a temptation to look down when you are nervous but try to resist it. Be interested in the interviewer, notice their appearance. Not only is it useful for you to be able to recognise them when next you meet but also it will give you valuable clues about their personality, and make sure your head is up.

Don't smoke unless you're offered a cigarette. It may calm your nerves but it's apt to infuriate non-smokers, or even more so those who are trying to give up. Remember to shake hands when you leave, be sure to include everyone in your farewell, the spectators often have as much say in the final decision as the person who conducts the interview.

Make it easier for yourself by keeping bags and accessories to a minimum. It's almost impossible to negotiate exits and entrances burdened with several carrier bags, an overcoat and an umbrella. If there is a hurricane raging outside or you must go on a shopping spree before the interview, leave your belongings in reception.

## Controlling nervous tension

This is a more difficult problem to tackle. Controlling the kind of unconscious nervous gestures and mannerisms most of us make when we're under stress is difficult at the best of times, let alone during an interview. Unfortunately, not only do they distract, they also increase our physical tension. Although it may take some time and practice it is worth combating them. First of all find out what they are. It can be difficult to observe this for yourself, so ask a close friend to be brutally honest and point them out to you. Armed with the knowledge, try to start to catch yourself out. This can be tricky; they're obviously going to occur when you are under pressure. However, if you have prior warning of a situation that could be potentially stressful, prepare yourself ahead of time and consciously counteract the action whatever it might be. For example, make sure your hands are free if you customarily clasp them, release the muscles in your forehead if you have a tendency to frown, etc. If you can successfully resist the urge just once, you are well on the way to conquering the habit. At first you will feel very vulnerable but you will soon notice that, as you release the muscles involved, the rest of your body will relax as well. The next time it will be a little easier to notice and control, until gradually your body learns that this particular reaction to tension is no longer necessary.

It is also a good idea to practice some form of relaxation technique. There are so many available, from the tried and tested such as the Alexander Technique, yoga and meditation, to the newer (if only to the West) chanting techniques (for more details see page 122). Experiment until you find the one that suits you best. Be sure to leave time before you set off for the interview and have at least a quarter of an hour's relaxation. It's important to relax the body and clear the mind before you get there; it will then be much easier to cope with the inevitable nerves when they start to plague you. There's a section dealing with nerves in the chapter on sight-reading but here are a few additional tips.

Having spent time relaxing the body before leaving for the interview, on the way there watch vigilantly that the tension doesn't creep back. This can be very hard when you are dealing with traffic or public transport but it's worth the effort. If the body can stay free the mind is less likely to become obsessed with exploring all the possible disasters that could lie ahead. When you arrive resist the temptation to be drawn into conversation before going into the interview. Some people misguidedly think that they can alleviate nerves by chatting, but this acts as a further stimulant to an already racing mind. If you meet a friend there, arrange to go for a gossip after the casting session.

Don't underrate the power of 'hyping' yourself up, whether it be by repeating a phrase such as 'I deserve this job' or listing to yourself all your assets and talents. Positive thinking does work and it's certainly more constructive than dwelling on all your faults and past ill fortune. Lastly and most important of all, remember to *keep breathing out*.

## Coping with rejection

Coping with rejection is not easy. But always keep in mind that it isn't personal failure. There are so many people up for every job no one can succeed every time: there are always going to be factors beyond your control. The actor before you may have fitted the director's image of the part exactly, or the star has insisted that his girlfriend play the role that you went up for, etc., etc. You have to accept that disappointment is an inevitable aspect of the profession. You will keep your self-respect and confidence if you can come out of an interview knowing that you have handled the situation well and that you have given of your best. And remember there is always the chance that the director or casting director will use you in another part at a later date.

# 4

# *Sight-reading*

The ability to sight-read well is an essential skill for any actor. It has become a vitally important stage in the casting process for all branches of the media. Once launched into the profession you will seldom be called upon to perform an audition speech as such, whereas sight-reading or 'reading for a part' has become almost mandatory. Even well-established players are prepared to read when meeting a director who is new to them or when seeking a part outside their usual range. Yet this standard requirement is regarded with dread by many experienced as well as aspiring actors. It needn't be. The terror can be overcome and the ordeal made even enjoyable if you approach it with the right attitude and arm yourself with a secure technique.

## The attitude

Let's look at this fearful task. Why are you being asked to read anyway? What is required of you?

- To display your talents as an actor.
- To demonstrate your suitability for the role.
- To indicate your understanding and sense of identification with the part.

In short you are expected to perform. Not a polished in-depth performance that only comes after intensive work in rehearsals, but your spontaneous response to the text. You are an actor being given a chance to show what you can do.

What is *not* wanted is a fluent, precise, speedy and glib enunciation of the words on the page. They know the script, it's your interpretation of it they are interested in.

If you haven't had a chance to see the script beforehand and have been asked to read it 'cold' (a term used to describe reading a script out loud having never seen it before), always ask for a chance to read it through to yourself first. It is unusual for you to be refused. If you are, it will be because the viewers want a completely spontaneous reaction to the text and will make allowances for the inevitable stumbles and misreadings.

Remember, take your time. While you are reading you are in control of the situation, you are giving the performance. They want to enjoy it – after all they do want to find the right person for the role.

## The technique

**1. Approaching the text**   When approaching any text for the first time always obey the golden rule, 'start with yourself'. In the case of sight-reading, it is imperative. There isn't time for probing exploration of the character's personality. It has to be you, you must identify with it completely. If you have been given the script ahead of time, read it slowly, taking it phrase by phrase. Think of feeling your way through it rather than reading. Don't worry about the words, your brain will absorb them automatically as you go, concentrate on the thoughts and emotions. Use your imagination to find out what you would have to feel like in order to say each line and mean it. What changes of thoughts and emotions would you have to undergo to link one phrase with the next? This way, you are playing each moment as it comes without anticipation and as truthfully as possible with the information you have. Even if you have to read cold, you can apply this technique. You may have to take more time finding the thoughts and emotional changes and you may get yourself trapped in some unintentional 'dead ends', but you will be given advice on how you can avoid this in the following paragraphs.

If you are given the script beforehand you will have time to prepare and map out the emotional journey of the scene or speech. This is much easier to remember than trying to learn the words. You set in your mind what the character is feeling moment by moment during the piece, note the changes of emotional gear, notice where the feelings become particularly highly charged, in other words the climatic points in the dialogue. It is a good idea to mark them with a pencil as you go along – this helps to secure them in your mind, and makes the text easier to play when the time comes. You can see where you build emotionally and where you must give yourself time to find the next thought or feeling. It also helps you to cover if you lose your place in the script. If you know what the character is feeling you have something to play while you search for the line. Remember to be greedy, to look for as many changes of thought and emotion as possible. The more you have to play, the less nervous and the more confident you will be.

In addition, as outlined in the chapter on auditions, there are four important questions that have to be answered before you start to read the dialogue aloud, regardless of whether you have had time to prepare it or are reading it cold. For our purposes we have called them the four 'W' questions, and the advice below relates to the sight-reading answers to these questions.

*What has happened before the speech begins?* What circumstances have led up to this moment in the character's life? In the case of sight-reading, when time and information is usually limited, the answer has to be simple and straightforward as there isn't time for in-depth analysis when you are sight-reading. It is enough to know your character's state of mind and body, where the scene is set and what has just occurred. This is one advantage you will have if you have to read cold. You will be able to find out these facts from the director or casting director when they hand you the script. If you have been lucky enough to have been given a whole script beforehand, there will of course be no problem as you will have time to read it through and gain all the information you need. If, however, as usually happens, you receive only the 'sides' (pages of script) which contain just your part, you have to base your answer on whatever you can glean from the dialogue you have got and use your imagination to fill in any holes.

Don't worry too much if this turns out to be the case. The important thing is not to get it 'right' but to make a decision that will provide you with an emotional starting point. In the unlikely event of your getting it horribly wrong, most directors or casting directors would be understanding and spend time discussing the actual circumstances with you, especially if your reading has sincerity and conviction.

The other three questions can be addressed together.

*What are you doing?* This can be broken down to a single active verb, i.e. I explain, I apologise, I complain, etc.

*Who are you talking to?* This question appears to be easy to answer but involves your deciding on the relationship between yourself and the other character.

*What do you need?* Every action we take is motivated by a need. You have to decide what you want or expect back in response to what you are about to say. You won't have time to agonise over finding the 'right' answers. Make a decision based on your immediate response to the text. The purpose of the questions in this instance is to provide you with focus and conviction and prevent your resorting to generalised emotion. Too often actors, in an attempt to feel more secure, try to get an angle on the scene by categorising it under an emotional heading, such as, he or she is angry, or frightened, or bewildered, etc. This can only result in a generalisation of the feelings involved and a tendency to use received ideas and responses rather than trusting to their own creative intuition. Once you have made your decisions you will be armed with an emotional starting point and a purpose. When you start to perform, remember you are the character – don't be inhibited, give yourself over to the speech, let the emotional changes take you with them and play it for all you are worth.

These then are the main guidelines to follow when approaching the text. However, there are some techniques and hints which can make the task a lot easier. For example, the text itself can disclose a lot more information about the scene and the role beyond just its meaning, if you know how to look for it. The layout, punctuation and choice of words can give you immediate indications of the scene's content and the character's mood, situation, status and even personality traits.

**2. The layout**   The appearance of the text can give you clues on the playing and the emotional structure of the scene. Even at a glance the shape of the dialogue on the page will tell you something about the character and their situation, if only in broad terms.

For instance, if your lines are a series of short responses, this will denote a degree of uncertainty or an unwillingness to expound freely. If this is then followed by a longish speech you would be safe in assuming this is likely to be an explanation or outburst of pent-up emotion. If, on the other hand, your dialogue is limited to brief utterances this will indicate that your character's situation or their personality makes them disinclined to express their feelings easily through speech. By the same token if the part is mainly made up of fairly long speeches this demonstrates that they are comfortable with language and have a need to verbalise thoughts and feelings. A long speech often takes the form of a narrative or story. If so, be careful not to build too quickly. If you had a chance to read through the script beforehand remember where the climatic points are. If you are reading cold try to look ahead and check how long the speech lasts so you can pace yourself accordingly.

With any long speech there are some points to be aware of, as mentioned earlier in the chapter on auditions. Nobody plans to make a long speech in normal conversation, they just happen to you. We go on speaking because either nobody interrupts us or because we keep thinking of more things we want to say. It's important to play this, really find those changes of thought.

Dialogue sometimes contains broken sentences, and they can be quite difficult to deal with. If your line is written as a broken sentence always complete it. Don't wait hoping the other person will come in; if they don't you're going to be the one who looks foolish. If you are the one who interrupts it is an indication of your character's state of mind – they are excited for some reason. In order to portray this you must break in even if you've lost your place in the script. Ad lib, improvise, but keep up the emotional impetus.

Indicated pauses also need careful treatment. They obviously signify a moment of deep thought or extreme tension but in the context of sight-reading you have to be sure they will hold. Unless you have really built up to them they can become awkward and unreal. If you are in any doubt cut them short.

**3. Words**   Apart from the obvious indications words give of the character's environment, status and personality, as with an indigenous accent, a stylised form of speech or particular choice of words (a character whose every second utterance is an expletive is clearly not an aesthete), there are more subtle points to be noted and effectively used.

Adjectives are worth attention. Remember they are

there because we want to show what we feel about the noun in question. So really use them in the sense of injecting them with that feeling. They also need to be 'found'. Don't let them fall too trippingly off the tongue. Not only is it more realistic – in life we search for the right word to express exactly what we mean – but also it gives you time as a sight-reader to look ahead a bit and catch your breath. Words that are unusual or hard to pronounce also need to be pointed. Don't pass over them quickly as if they were unexceptional. Unless your character is singularly well educated and eloquent they will be special to them. Take time to find the word and pronounce it carefully or consciously as you would in life.

Repetition of words can be important. If your character repeats a word, especially one used shortly before, it means that there must be some reason for it, if only unconsciously, so you must slightly stress it. Similarly, if a word is repeated from another character's lines this must be subtly demonstrated.

The use of names can be significant. We rarely address anyone by name unless for a specific reason: to draw their attention, to denote respect, disapproval or superiority, etc. Decide which it is in the given context and play it.

**4. The kind of words your character uses**   This can give you clues to their personality. Do they like using long words, showing them off whenever possible? Are their sentences concise and to the point, even within long speeches, or do they meander and waffle? Start to look for these details and you will be surprised how soon you begin to pick up and notice verbal idiosyncrasy. Words can also act as a helpful guide to finding your place again after having raised your head to deliver a line or engage with the person who is reading with you. If you pinpoint the word ahead and its place on the page before you lift your eyes, you will then return easily to exactly the right place when you want to continue reading. This sounds more complicated than it is, it becomes quite simple with a little practice.

**5. Punctuation**  Punctuation is the sight-reader's guide and friend but you have to know how to interpret it and use it to your advantage. The accepted rule of pausing for the relevant amount of time at every full stop, colon and comma for example, can be misleading. It is more useful to think of them as changes of gear in a train of thought. A full stop can indicate not only the completion of a thought or a signal that a response is expected, but also a stage in the development of a continued thought. Commas are often misused and overplayed as pauses, it is wiser and more effective when sight-reading to use them as a guide to slight shifts in the flow of thought.

Exclamation marks and question marks are self-explanatory but colons and semicolons require a more subtle approach, standing as they do between the full stop and the comma and, as such, can be very useful. They obviously denote a greater change in the pattern of thought than does the comma and thus provide you with a convenient resting place – a moment to recharge emotionally, find the impetus to carry on the thought and, of course, take a sneaky look at the lines head. In fact they can be a more valuable pausing point than a full stop. They are less obvious and if you end with an upward inflection before you take the pause, you can afford to take a longer rest by using it as search for thought or a moment of emotional recovery. Pauses at full stops need care. Unless you are absolutely sure it is the end of a thought, it's best not to pause too long: it can sound unreal and too conciously 'read'. This is not to suggest that you ignore full stops – they need their due recognition – but don't play them as endings or the completion of an idea without making sure that is what they really signify.

Another trick, which must be used only in emergencies, when you have hopelessly lost your cool and need to take a deep breath to collect yourself, is to start a sentence swiftly on the back of the last, ignoring the full stop but pausing after the first word in the new sentence. This must be used with great discretion and only in dire necessity because it can sound false and tricksy if over-used.

**6. Coping with fluffs**   Remember, it's the flow of thought that is important not the flow of words. Once you launch into the dialogue, you are that person. When the inevitable fluffs and misreadings occur, don't panic, stutter and re-read the phrase again or, worse still, look up and apologise. Stay in character and play one of the following, whichever seems appropriate.

- Re-think the phrase or word before reiterating it.
- Pause while you search for the right word.
- Pretend the stumble was due to agitation or an over eagerness to get the words out.

Similarly if you lose your place. Remain calm while you find it again, then take a beat before starting. When you do, play it as though you have lost your train of thought and that you are thinking what to say next.

Begin to notice how often in life people stammer over words, forget what they're saying in mid-sentence or use odd or inappropriate inflections. You will see that it happens all the time and you will become less inhibited about any stumbles you might make, and at the same time build up a useful repertoire of realistic recoveries.

**7. Stage directions**   As a general rule these are to be ignored when you are sight-reading unless they refer to your character's reaction to a situation. Even then use them as a guide and with discretion. If they say 'she bursts into tears', or 'he laughs hysterically', obviously you can use them but something as ambiguous as 'he stiffens' or 'her look darkens' are best avoided.

**8. Voice**   The vocal demands will vary depending on the emotional content of the scene and the background and environment of the character; however, there are some fundamental points that are helpful to keep in mind.

a. Don't 'put on' a voice. This doesn't refer to an accent but to any distortion of your natural voice that limits its range or constitutes a vocal mannerism in order to convey character. This can only be used when you are completely conversant with the role and the text and when you are absolutely sure that it is an essential ingredient of the character's personality. In the context of sight-reading it will only succeed in spoiling the reality and sincerity that comes when you approach a new text with an open mind and a free voice. Even when the part requires the use of an accent you need to be careful that in your eagerness to get it accurate the accent doesn't becomes the sum total of the characterisation.

b. Keep your sentences vocally open-ended – this is perhaps the most useful tip of all when it comes to sight-reading. As noted above, don't make final statements unless you are quite sure the train of thought is completely finished, keep the thought going on. This may entail using an upward inflection, but as a too conscious use of them can lead to an affected delivery it is safer to think of strongly playing the thought that carries you from one line to another and/or its subtext. This way you are less likely to get trapped into a wrong inflection or having to make an awkward and unreal mental leap into the next sentence.

c. Let the voice move. Either through nerves or mistaken notion of realism actors supress their voice's natural response to changes of thought and emotional intensity. Dare to let the voice reach the extreme notes at either end of your range especially in moments of intense emotion. Remember that each change of thought and emotion has its own vocal energy and pitch. Make sure you are freeing the voice sufficiently for it to communicate this.

### Controlling and harnessing those nerves

How many times have actors complained, 'It would have gone so much better if I hadn't been so nervous,' on their return from an audition or interview. In fact, they are wrong. It wasn't the nerves that were at fault but their handling of them. In reality, nerves can be an asset. It is your attitude towards them that determines whether they work for you or against you. You want to learn how to master them rather than drive them away completely. The flow of adrenalin that they cause can invest your performance with sparkle and edge if used well instead of reducing it to quavering uncertainty. In fact the minute you acknowledge the possibility that they could be of value and that you might even welcome their presence, you immediately begin to empower yourself. You have taken the first step in bringing them under your control.

Another way of dealing with nerves is purely practical: some simple physical exercises to relax the parts of the body that are most vulnerable to nervous tension. Unfortunately, they are the very ones you need under control in order to be able to sight-read or even speak efficiently.

**1. The respiratory system** (which is just a grand way of saying the breath) This is the most crucial area of all. If the breath is restricted it immediately affects the whole body, and if you can't breathe freely and deeply you haven't a hope of relaxing the rest of the body. When you are nervous, the body responds at once by shortening and reducing your intake of breath. You will notice if you are very frightened, you virtually hold your breath and breathe in little gasps. You must counteract this as soon as possible by breathing out heavily. If the tension is extreme you may have to do this forcibly a couple of times – not too often or you will become giddy. Once you have emptied the lungs the body is compelled to inhale deeply. Ignore the inward breath – it will take care of itself. Just concentrate on letting the breath go. You will notice that the rate of breathing will automatically begin to slow down. Continue consciously to release the outward breath but making the exhalations increasingly gentle until the breath is flowing freely and rhythmically. You will find that as the breath calms, the body becomes more relaxed and the brain clears. You've given it something to occupy it other than tormenting you with reminders of how nervous you are.

When you know you are going to enter a situation which will make you nervous, be vigilant, monitor the body, and as soon as you feel it begin to tense up, release the breath by sighing out. This way you can prevent the breath becoming severely restricted. Keep it under control by continuing to sigh out gently but firmly at regular intervals. You can even do this while you are waiting to go into an audition or interview.

**2. The jaw**   This is important because a tense jaw can affect the tongue, mouth, cheeks and the larynx, in fact all your speech organs.

Start by unclenching your teeth. If you are relaxed they should be slightly apart behind a barely closed mouth. Now let go the tongue, think of relaxing it right back to the root which is way back at the top of the throat on a line with the bottom of the chin. You should feel the mouth and lower cheeks soften. A trick which enables you to release the jaw and mouth quickly and surreptitiously is to roll your tongue back to the soft palate. The teeth will automatically part and the jaw and mouth relax. Return the tongue to its resting place behind the lower teeth leaving everything else in its new free position. Like the breath the jaw needs constant watching as it is one of the first places to tighten up when you are tense. Luckily it is an easy and quick way to relax if you use this method.

**3. The throat muscles**  These are not so easy to control. If you have been taught the 'yawn' or 'smile' exercises they can be helpful; if not try the following routine. As you breathe out think of breathing out through the muscles round the larynx. On the next outward breath imagine that the back of the mouth opens up into a huge cavern, then with the mouth a little apart, articulate a few voiceless 'Ka' sounds. Pay particular attention to the downward movement of the back of the tongue. Try to keep the space between the tongue and the soft palate as large and free as possible. Visualise the breath flowing freely through the space at the back of the mouth as you breathe out. This exercise, although it needs concentration, can help to combat the tendency for the throat to close when you are nervous.

**4. The face**  Unless you are extremely self-confident you have to be alone for this exercise. Simply massage your face with the tips of your fingers. Pay particular attention to the centre of the forehead, the eyebrows, the cheeks and around the mouth, making little circular movements, moving the skin over the surface of the facial bones. It will feel wonderful.

**5. The body**  Well, you can hardly prostrate yourself on the floor of the reception area and practice a full body relaxation, but there is a trick that will help release tension. Think of your feet and hands being heavy. When you walk really feel your weight on the floor, think down into it. When we are nervous we tense our legs and feet to such an extent we almost walk an inch above the ground. Similarly with the arms and hands, the shoulders rise up in tension and the poor hands just dangle there rather clammily. While you are sitting waiting to be called into the interview or whatever, imagine that the hands and arms are becoming heavier and heavier and that the palms are growing warm, then release the wrists and slowly circle them. Finally take your arms up and gently massage the back of your neck – be careful, usually a lot of tension builds up here. It can feel quite tender. Then think of breathing out through those tense muscles. It really helps to let them go.

**6. The mind**  No miracles here I'm afraid. Yet there are a few tips which can persuade the brain to stop torturing you for a while. Apart from anything else it will be so busy taking you through the previous exercises it won't have much time left to dwell on all the dreadful possibilities. Simple visualisation can be useful. Imagine yourself entering the interview room calmly yet with interested anticipation. Take yourself in your imagination, through the entire interview with as successful a result as you could possibly wish for. This really can help to put you in the right frame of mind. Alternatively, remind yourself of how talented you are; how right for the part and that you are the actor that *they* have been waiting to meet. Think of all the reasons why you would be ideal for the role.

You know yourself that even when you are very upset you will forget the problem for a while in spite of yourself if something really interesting or intriguing happens. It is a good principle to bear in mind.

Lastly, getting those nerves to work with you. Just think how good you feel when you are excited: you know you look your best, your mind is alert, there is a spring in your step and all seems right with your world. Now think about those symptoms. Believe it or not, they are the same as the nervous apprehension you feel before an important interview or audition: the same adrenalin flow, the same butterflies in the stomach, the same anticipation of the unknown. Only your conviction that things are going to be dreadful rather than pleasurable is at variance. All you have to do is dare to think that the unknown experience ahead might turn out to be enjoyable, to convert those feelings from fear to excitement. It's easier than you think, especially armed with your repertoire of relaxation exercises (see page 122). And it is certainly worth a try.

## Confidence

Confidence comes with knowledge and practice. Now you know about the techniques of sight-reading so it's time for the practice. Sight-reading is a skill and, as with any skill, once you have learned the basic techniques it is only by continual practice that it becomes easy, and ultimately, almost second nature to you. This is particularly true of sight-reading because when you use it professionally, it will nearly always be in situations that are stressful and demanding.

Make a habit of reading aloud to yourself, daily if possible to begin with. Start with material you know and relate to easily, using the advice and techniques in this chapter. Once you are familiar with them and begin to feel a little more secure, start to have fun, play around with the material. Really use the words, dare to overplay them, experiment vocally, discover the different effects you can achieve with your voice, the infinite variety and subtle possibilities that are available to you through changes of pitch, pace and volume. Then begin to stretch yourself further. Choose plays and roles that you think you will never have a chance of playing. Set up play-reading sessions with fellow actors, hear each other and exchange friendly and helpful criticism. You will be surprised how soon you become an accomplished sight-reader and how much you enjoy yourself.

After all, sight-reading is just another chance to do what you like best – acting.

Finally, perhaps the most valuable words of advice. When you are at the casting and about to start reading, cut off from your surroundings, forget everything and everybody except the person you are reading with, really engage with the character and just go for it.

# 5

# *What to Expect*

## *Drama school entrance auditions*

For most people this will be their first experience of an audition. If you have read the earlier chapters of this book you will have begun to realise that this needn't be a traumatic event, especially if you are:

- well prepared
- sure of what you want, in this case from the course
- have some idea what to expect from the audition

The first point has been covered in the chapters dealing with audition speeches and interview techniques. The second is a matter of spending time to consider the answers to the following questions. Why do you want to go on the course? What do you expect to gain from it? And what kind of theatrical training would be most beneficial for your particular talents and aspirations, i.e. physical theatre, text based, or one where there is a greater emphasis on song and dance? You may feel impatient or confused at having to make the decision, before you have even started the course, but whether you make the right decision is not all that important, there is invariably a chance to change direction within most drama schools. What matters is that, by asking yourself these questions, your attitude towards the situation will have subtly changed. You are now approaching the audition with a view to assess as well as being assessed. It is also a good idea to frame a few questions you would like to ask about the course. There is often time set aside to interview auditioners and it's impressive if you can contribute instead of just remaining passive.

The last point (about what you can expect from an audition) will be dealt with in the rest of this section.

When you apply to the school or college you will usually receive information on the type of speech or speeches you are expected to prepare. You may also receive a schedule of the audition. For many courses this may involve singing and movement sessions – the format will naturally vary but there are essential components that are common to them all.

You will perform your speeches in front of more than one person. This obviously makes for a fairer assessment of your work but it does mean that they may confer and take notes during your performance – don't be put off. An accompaniment of rustling papers and murmuring voices doesn't mean they are not paying attention or that they are bored. The notes are just reminders to help when they come to make the final decision and the comments can be favourable.

You may have an audience of fellow candidates. Don't let this inhibit you either. They will be far too nervous about their own performance to be interested in criticising yours. In fact it is much more common that a degree of sympathy and support builds up between the auditionees, uniting them against what is seen to be the dreadful scrutiny of the viewers.

## The song

If you are an experienced and talented singer you can happily skip this section; you will probably sail through this portion of the audition without a qualm. If, however, like many of us, the idea of singing in public fills you with a horror comparable to that suffered while awaiting medieval torture, then read on. Here are a few words of advice and comfort.

Firstly, unless you are auditioning for a musical theatre course, you would not fail the audition just because you can't carry a tune or hold a note. Then why do we have to undergo the ordeal, you may justifiably ask. Well, they want to check your potential in case you turn out to be a fledgling Barbra Streisand and don't know it. In reality most people can improve their singing voice immeasurably with correct training. They have started a course convinced they couldn't sing, to find at the end of it not only that they could, but that their first job on leaving was in a musical. Even those who haven't got what is termed 'a good voice' can learn to put over a song. At this moment that is what you should aim for.

Apart from assessing your singing voice the auditioners are looking to see how well you can communicate your personality to an audience. It can sometimes happen that an untrained actor's talent and ability to respond to an audience become more apparent when he is singing than when he is performing a speech. Through nerves and an anxiety to succeed they stifle all spontaneity. Approach the song as you would a speech, choose one that you think suits your personality and where you can relate to the words and sentiments, where the tune is limited to the notes in the middle of your vocal range (those you can reach without strain or effort) and where the rhythm is straightforward.

As a general rule it is best to steer clear of pop songs or rock and roll numbers as they are very difficult to put over live without the proper equipment and backing. Hours are spent in the recording studio with sophisticated equipment in order to produce the finished result that we hear. Songs from musical shows are safer if you avoid those that demand an exceptional vocal range. *Little Shop of Horrors, Miss Saigon, Starlight Express* and *South Pacific* for instance, all contain a number of songs that are easy to sing but with a strong narrative which gives you a chance to use your acting ability in order to put them over. Folksongs and old music hall songs are also a useful source of material.

Having decided on your choice, sing it as if it were a piece of dialogue. Imagine the person you are addressing it to. While you are learning the words, notice the climatic points as you would with a speech – in fact approach the whole task in a similar way as you would an audition speech; in other words – act it. When you have worked out how you want to play it, practise, practise, practise. The more insecure you feel about singing the more you must practise, especially in front of other people. Bribe your friends, family and enemies if necessary but reach a stage when you feel confident enough to sing it in front of anyone, anywhere, then have fun with it. Ignore any bum notes and enjoy selling the song to them.

Finally a word about musical accompaniment. If at all possible rehearse at least a couple of times with an accompanist. There will be a pianist at the audition and it's very much easier to use them rather than try to sing a cappella or to a previously recorded tape. Remember to take the sheet music with you, making sure it is in the correct key for you. Pianists don't like being asked to transpose at a moment's notice. Also bear in mind that sheet music is for them, not you! You will perform the song without any such aids. You should try to convey the impression that the words have just sprung spontaneously into your mind in spite of all those weeks of practice.

## Improvisation

For those who have never done any acting improvisation here is an attempt at a brief explanation of what to expect – an attempt because, frankly, there seems to be as many different types of improvisations as there are directors. The only obvious common denominator is that they are unprepared. You have no idea beforehand what you will be asked to do. It is unlikely to involve any work with a script but apart from that you must be ready for nearly anything from games to emotional recall (recalling moments of extreme emotion from your own experience). But it is enjoyable. It is being able to act and react with complete freedom rather as a child plays at make believe.

Improvisation sessions are often included in the audition schedule. It's important to remember their purpose. There are many experienced actors who panic when called upon to improvise, forgetting that its aim is to encourage a free imaginative response to a given situation and to other actors without the restrictions imposed by a script or set moves. In other words it's supposed to remove inhibitions rather than arouse them. In this context it is also used to gauge how open and receptive you are to direction. Knowing this you will realise that you don't have to rack your brains for clever ideas. Just listen carefully to what is proposed and act upon your initial response to the given idea and let it take on its own momentum. Often the simplest ideas develop into the most exciting and effective impros.

## The interview

An acting interview is not quite like any other job interview in that the emphasis is mainly on you rather than your experience or qualifications. It will be your personality, your opinions, your reactions – and your ability to communicate these – that will interest the interviewer. Once you are a fully fledged actor the ability to handle these situations well will be crucial – they are an essential part of the casting process. In this instance, however, those interviewing will make allowances for your lack of experience and sympathise with your inevitable nervousness. An interview, in fact, is nothing more than a slightly more formal chat between you and one or more others. (It is very unusual to be interviewed by more than three people.)

The advice given in Chapter 3 on interviews will be helpful, but here are a few additional points with particular relevance to this situation.

At some colleges and schools there is a policy to interview only those they have short-listed for consideration but this is not always the case. In any event it is as well to be prepared. They will ask you questions about your background, any theatrical experience you might have had and why you want to act. Enthusiasm tempered with determination and an awareness of your goals and ambitions are qualities that will impress on this occasion. It's worthwhile thinking out possible answers to likely but more awkward questions such as: Why do you want to act? Why this course and not another? What do you feel you have to offer as an actor? Do you think you can withstand the inevitable rejections and disappointments that are a part of theatrical life? These are all frequently posed and it's easier to answer them fully if you have had time to think about them beforehand. Obviously you don't want to recite your answers parrot-fashion but having a general idea of how you might reply helps to focus your mind and give you confidence.

This is also your opportunity to ask your questions concerning the course. Few interviewers will not be delighted with intelligent questions; it shows evidence of a lively mind and a sense of responsibility for your own future.

## Nerves

The chapters on the interview and sight-reading feature sections on how to cope with nerves, see pages 55 and 68. Read them through and try to put the advice into practice. Remember all the other auditionees will be suffering the same horror and that the auditioners are human beings not monsters; in fact, many of them are actors or ex-actors and understand only too well the agony you are experiencing.

## The result

For once the saying 'no news is good news' really does hold true. Some schools tell you immediately if you have failed to get in, others deliver the bad news within a few weeks. The good news can take somewhat longer and the outcome is not always straightforward. You may be fortunate enough to receive an unconditional 'yes' within a week or two or you may be recalled for a further audition or interview, or you may be placed on a reserve list. In the latter case it is not unknown for students to be notified of the result a week before the term is due to start, although this is unusual. If you have not heard within a month or so and time is running out it is worth ringing up to find out what the situation is. Applicants have even managed to tip the balance in their favour by charming the school secretary.

## *TV casting*

Today television provides most actors with the majority of their work. The term television, however, covers so many different types and opportunities of employment, from plays, series, sitcoms, soap operas to pop videos (the list is endless). The money is good, the audience vast, and there's always the chance of instant stardom. A successful interview for a leading part in a new series and you could be a household name within a few months. But it can be hard to make that initial break-through into this section of the media. To be honest, it is unlikely that you will get the chance of going up for a TV part unless you have representation. Casting directors who have seen and admire an actor's work may put them up for a part, but they really prefer to work through an agent. Occasionally there are ads in the weekly casting publications but these are generally for actors with special skills, and that means extremely special skills, such as concert standard violinists, or young female karate champions!

These observations hold true for both the United States and the United Kingdom. Indeed the principles that lie behind the casting procedures in both countries are very similar, but there are some differences in the methods used.

Let's start with the United Kingdom. Here you will be given the date, time and place of the casting by your agent, but sometimes any actual information about the part can be limited. 'It's a young girl/man, darling, about your age. A nice part. I think you go all the way through' – can be all the information you get to go on. If this is the case it's worth making yourself unpopular with your agent at this point and pressing for more details. Remember the advice given in Chapter 1. Those at the interview are expecting you to be well prepared and blaming your agent for your failure is not considered an acceptable excuse. In fact it is never wise to criticise your agent at an interview unless they have made a major blunder because most are on friendly terms with the casting directors and it will only reflect badly on you.

This is also your opportunity to carry out the advice given by Matthew Robinson in Chapter 1 and find out for yourself as much as you can about the director, the writer, the producer, the script itself and anything else that could be helpful at the interview. You may or may not be sent 'sides' (pages of the script) ahead of time, depending on the size of your part, the amount of clout your agent has with the production company or availability of the script. If not, set off with high hopes and an open mind.

The venue may vary in size and grandeur, from the huge office blocks owned by the big companies (such as the BBC Television Centre) to a small office in Soho, but the format is essentially the same. On arrival you will go to a reception area where you will be handed the sides.

As you go to sit down you may notice one or two people of the same sex and a similar age as yourself engrossed in the identical pages of script. They are the competition. Avoid making any negative comparison like 'they look so much more attractive, calmer and experienced than me'. They are probably not and you don't know what is wanted anyway. The only problem they present is that, as this is your first glimpse of the script, their presence may disturb your concentration. Until you are a really confident and accomplished sight-reader, it is much easier to assimilate the script if you are alone. If you are finding it very difficult, it is worth seeking out the nearest toilet to secure a little privacy and maybe even read it out loud, if you can brave the curious looks that might be waiting for you when you emerge from the cubicle from those wanting to use it for more orthodox reasons. Either way, allow yourself plenty of time to read it through thoroughly and put into practice the techniques and advice given in Chapter 4 on sight-reading before you are due to go in for the interview.

When you are summoned into the office you will be faced with two possible scenarios. Usually your agent will have warned you which one it will be, but as has been mentioned before, always be prepared for every eventuality: they could have got it wrong, there could have been a change of plan etc. In most cases the interview will be with the director and one or more of the production team. (These may be the producer, the casting director, the writer or the PA (the director's assistant.)) However, if you are unknown to the casting director, it is a large-scale production or you are auditioning to join a long running series, your first interview may be with the casting director alone who will then decide whether you should go through to meet the director. In either case you must be prepared for the fact that in all likelihood you will be filmed or taped during the meeting. This may take place when you are sight-reading (the most usual), while you are chatting or you may have been asked to learn the script beforehand, ready to give a mini performance for the camera at the interview. This practice of putting artists on film or tape for reference used to occur only at auditions for films, but with the advent of cheaper and easy-to-use technology such as camcorders, it is becoming more and more part of the casting process. The point is to remain calm and unruffled when the ubiquitous camera is produced. Whether the interview is with the casting director or the director it will follow along the same general lines. Invariably they will start by asking you a few questions about yourself, followed by a summary of the plot and a brief outline of the role. After this you are generally asked to read. Occasionally this routine is reversed and you have to read before being interviewed. There are also instances when the session consists only of an interview. This last possibility can be for several reasons.

- They know your work already (very flattering this).
- The part is too small for sight-reading to serve any useful purpose.
- This is a preliminary interview to be followed by another where you will be called upon to read if you are under consideration for the part.
- The director is so experienced (such as Herbie Wise) that he feels he can base his decision purely on the interview (very unusual).

You will read with either the director or the casting director. Whoever it might be you must play solely to them, really engage with them, forget everyone else in the room until you have finished reading. Afterwards, the director may work with you on the script and sometimes let you have another go at it. Many actors think that the longer the time the director devotes to you, the more likely it is that the outcome will be favourable. However, although you may feel that you've been given a better chance to do yourself justice, there is no evidence to prove that this theory is correct. It is much more to do with a personal foible of the director and you are just as likely to get a part after a ten-minute interview as you are after an hour-long stint.

The affair usually ends with a few pleasantries. Try not to read too much into these. Interpreting 'See you soon' or 'We'll get back to you' as a promise of an imminent contract can only lead to disappointment. Be sure to include everyone in your farewell – any one of them could tip the balance in your favour.

In the United States the sequence of events differs slightly. There is a greater likelihood of getting the sides beforehand. Also, your agent will usually give you a good deal more information about the role and you will nearly always be interviewed by the casting agent first. If there is time the session will start with a brief chat, but normally you read straightaway and this will be videoed. This is even more important in the United States than in Britain because there are usually many more actors up for each part. For example in the pilot season* when actors are literally in and out within minutes, it would be impossible for any casting director, however diligent, to keep every one of them fresh in their mind after days of casting. This way your performance will be assessed at leisure and is more likely to receive attentive consideration.

If you are considered suitable for the part, you will be recalled to meet the director and producer. In some cases, it may only be the producer because often the choice of director is not finalised until the last stages of casting. You will be asked to read and yet again this may be taped. Depending on the size of the part (the larger the part the more neurotic they are about making a decision and the more people are brought in to approve or disapprove of you) you may be called back

---

*The pilot season is a period early in the year when a great many one-off episodes of new series are filmed. These are then shown to the networks who choose those they will launch in the coming season. This obviously provides not only a welcome increase in the work available but a chance to become a household name, nation-wide.

any number of times before the final choice is made. The age and type of show also has some bearing on this. If the show is a long-established series, you may well be recalled to see how you match up with the other members of the cast, but they are unlikely to spend as much time making up their minds as do the producers of an untried or one-off show.

Whatever the process of casting, whether it be in the United States or the United Kingdom, there are certain factors that are common to all and for you to bear in mind.

- Prepare as well as possible beforehand.
- Learn all you can about the director, the script and, most importantly, your role.
- Make an imput into the proceedings – at an interview contribute actively to the conversation.
- Remember they want to find the right person for the part. Why shouldn't it be you?
- Read Doreen Jones' advice in Chapter 1, page 24.
- Don't count on anything until you've signed the contract

## *Film castings*

Maybe it is because the rewards can be so spectacular, the finances involved are so enormous and the final outcome so uncertain, but the demands that are sometimes made upon an actor when 'going up' for a movie role can be considerable. In the United Kingdom these can range from the formidable to the minimal. The venue also can vary wildly from the proverbial garret to the bridal suite in a luxury hotel. The time spent on the process may be less than half an hour or weeks of callbacks. In the United States, the procedure, although it is equally demanding, is at least a little more predictable. Let's start there and examine the idiosyncrasy of the British system later.

## The United States

Here you will receive the script before your appointment with the casting director, but when you get it varies from a day to several days beforehand. Strangely, the casting session for film is often much more relaxed than that for TV and, if they don't think you are right for the part, the casting director will normally tell you then and there rather than waste your time. If they consider that you might be suitable for the part, they will interview you briefly, and then read the script through with you. They often then take time to discuss the role with you and offer some direction before getting you to read again. This reading is usually put on tape. Should you be considered a possibility for the part you will be called in to meet the director or the producer fairly quickly. If they approve of what they see, they will ask you to read again and this will be taped. If you are then thought to be a strong contender for the part and it is an important one, they may arrange for you to take a proper screen test, in full make-up, etc. All this is heady stuff. You would have to be abnormally stoic not to get excited when the possibility of success is so near. The sense of rejection and disappointment if you don't then get the role can be devastating. Coping with these emotions is one of the greatest difficulties actors have to face. It can be even more demanding than the rigours of the castings.

## The United Kingdom

The diversity of the approach here is mainly due to geography and money. If the movie is an international production, the casting may be carried out in the United Kingdom while the director is abroad, perhaps finishing another film, and while the producers are based in another country. In these circumstances, it is common practice for the initial interviewing to be done by a casting director who then makes a short list of suitable actors. If your work is known to them you may be placed on the short list without any prior interview. Those who have been chosen are then put on tape and this is then forwarded to the relevant parties. This sounds like an efficient way of solving the problem and it probably is for all those involved – except for the actor. For them the experience can sometimes turn into an ordeal. In the best scenario, you will be given the sides a few days before, in the worst, a few hours or even, horror of horrors, when you arrive at the interview. You obviously have to learn the lines. You can hardly do yourself justice performing on camera with your head down and your eyes glued to the page. However, even in the very worse scenario you are given a little while to look at the script. Approach it as you would sight-reading. Remember that what they are looking for is your performance not the script. As long as you get the gist of it a few ad libs are not going to matter. When you go into the casting session you will be greeted by the casting director and a camera. Some kindly souls will let you rehearse the lines first, but don't count on it. There is a saying in the film industry 'Time is money' and certainly every stage of movie making, even casting, seems to reflect this, time is always at a premium.

Once the camera is turned on, you are on your own until the end of the scene. If you dry or 'fluff' your lines, still soldier on. Use the same techniques as with sight-reading: stay in character and bluff your way through. Normally, the casting director will read in the other parts but in some cases they have been known to sit in silence apparently oblivious to your need to be fed the lines. It's worth establishing before you begin as to whether they intend to do this or not, rather than discover the fact in the middle of the scene. If it is to be the case, your imagination will have to supply you with cues and responses. Sometimes you may be allowed another go, but, again don't rely on it.

The difficulty of performing in front of the camera in these circumstances and the thought that this performance on tape will decide whether you will get a chance to meet the director or even get the part is pretty chilling. But, comfort can be drawn from the fact that everyone else will be suffering from the same fate and that most directors realise how traumatic the experience can be. Foreknowledge of the worst that can happen will enable you to prepare well for the ordeal.

The more that you do it, the quicker you will find that you can learn the scripts and the easier the whole process becomes. Some actors even grow to enjoy it. After all, for once, you can do exactly as you like. The close-ups are all yours, you can conjure yourself up the most perfect co-star, in fact it could be fun.

## The low budget movie

With a low budget movie the set-up is far more casual. At the lowest end of the market you may find yourself being interviewed in the director's home or in the aforementioned garret office. This usually means that the film isn't fully financed yet and that they are paying for everything out of their own pockets. The interview is generally quite cosy and often just between you and the director. You will usually discuss the philosophy behind the project, the type of audience that they hope to interest as well as your part and its place in the storyline. In fact you will feel as if you are being really involved in the concept of the film. You may then be asked to read or return to do so at a later date. If you never hear from them again don't immediately put it down to your own failure. Sadly, all too often, many films just don't ever get made through lack of finance. On the other hand, when they do get the backing, they often turn out to be the most innovative and exciting films made, in many cases winning prizes at small film festivals and ending up being shown internationally.

## Movies made for the home market

As with the low budget movie, although ostensibly intended for home consumption, they have recently more frequently ended up being shown internationally. Further up the financial scale they will usually have a guaranteed financial backing and distribution, usually through one of the big TV companies. With secure finance comes a more formal approach to casting. For a start, they will have to employ a casting director who will select a short list of actors to meet and read with the director. It is quite usual for your first sight of the script to be when it is handed to you in the interview, so you will be able to make good use of all the tips in the chapter on sight-reading. Depending on the size of the part, the extent of your film experience and the size of the budget (as a general rule the larger the amount of money involved the greater the insecurities), this interview may be sufficient to decide whether or not you get the part. However, it is more usual to be recalled to read again and in some cases, when the part is large, you may be called back a number of times, either to read alone or with other actors, before a final decision is reached.

Although the essential ingredients remain the same there are a number of variations to this procedure which would be useful for you to know about.

1. You may be called in to meet the director and casting director together at the first interview.

2. If the director has flown in to the United Kingdom for the interviews they may take place in his hotel suite. You will usually wait downstairs in the hotel reception area before being ushered upstairs. He or she may well greet you wearing a dressing gown and you may find yourself being interviewed on a couch – but if this has led to anything untoward in recent years the actors and directors concerned have kept it to themselves because the reports back have been circumspect in the extreme.

3. Your first meeting with the casting director or director could entail your having to perform a section of the part on tape. This could mean that you would be given the script for the first time, be given a brief period to look at it and have to perform it then and there. Before you drop the page in horror and decide to forego your chance of international stardom here are some reassuring words.

- They won't expect you to be word perfect. Remember that it is you and your performance they want to see.
- You will be given time alone to work on the script.
- All your rivals for the part will be subjected to the same treatment.
- They will make allowances for stumbles, fluffs, etc.
- You are sometimes paired with another actor so you can lend each other support.

**To sum up**

In this branch of the industry, perhaps more than any other, there is still the chance of 'overnight success' and the audition process mirrors that. After weeks of recalls, screen tests and even promises from directors and producers, you may lose the job at the last minute. If you get the chance to play the role of your dreams and international recognition seems within your grasp, the film may fail to get a release or most of your part may end up on the cutting room floor. But if it works out, it can change your life completely. It does happen – there is still a possibility of sudden fame and fortune.

## Radio drama

A brief account here of the casting for radio drama. Brief because recently, with the demise of the BBC Radio Rep, finding work in this area has become much harder. Radio producers tend to cast from actors they already know or whose work they have seen or heard. You may occasionally obtain a casting through your agent if they have contacts in BBC drama. If so, the interview will usually entail meeting with the producer and or director and sight-reading with them from the script in question. While the basic tips on sight-reading apply, it is obviously important to remember that radio is an auditory medium. Your voice will have to do all the work so be sure that it is accurately expressing every change of thought and emotion. It would be sensible to listen to some radio drama beforehand and take note of the techniques used.

## Commercial castings

Commercials are an important source of income for any actor. In the United States particularly it can be extremely lucrative. Apart from the amounts earned by the so-called 'voice-over millionaires' and the fortunes paid to big names for endorsing products, there are the countless ads where actors portray other characters. Even if the initial fee for these is not enormous you stand to make a considerable sum from the repeat fees. This, of course, can vary depending on how widely they are shown but even those distributed in a limited area yield more than most theatre work. Many an actor has been saved from, if not starvation, at least eviction by the arrival of an unexpected cheque from a commercial they'd almost forgotten about. There are however, as with any fairy stories, ordeals to undergo before you reach the pot of gold. In this instance they come in the form of the castings. For those for whom commercial casting is a new experience the following paragraphs will we hope serve as guidance and perhaps prevent a few bruised egos.

Although there are specific agents dealing solely with commercials these are primarily for models. Most actors prefer to use their acting agent for both. Not only does it prevent a clash of interests but as many casting directors work on TV and films as well as commercials they have all the necessary contacts.

You will be given the details of your casting session by your agent in the usual way, but from then on the differences become apparent. Knowing about them will help you take them all in your stride.

To begin with, your appearance is of paramount importance. This does not mean that only those with exceptionally good looks will be considered, quite the contrary, it is the unusual or interesting face that is most likely to be chosen. When beauty is required they normally use a professional model.

Secondly, it's useful to know that the client (the manufacturer of the product or their PR) will have the final say on who gets the job. The director and the representative of the advertising agency, who will probably be present at the casting session, may offer their opinion but the ultimate veto remains with the client.

Realising these two facts will help you understand the somewhat cavalier treatment you may receive and the rapidity of the session.

On your arrival at reception you will be handed a form to fill in regarding your name, address, agent, vital statistics, etc. You may also be given a storyboard to study. This is a sheet of paper with pictures and dialogue rather like a comic strip, depicting the action of the commercial, shot by shot. It will show you any moves or dialogue that you may be required to perform.

When you enter the room or studio where the casting is being held, you will be greeted by the casting director who will introduce you to the others present. In the United Kingdom there will certainly be the director, and usually somebody from the advertising agency and the clients. The latter are unlikely to address you at all during the interview, they will oberve the proceedings, murmuring any comments to each other or the ad. man.

After greeting you, the director will ask you to give

your 'ID' on camera – this simply consists of your name and agent. This done, you will be required to stand full face and profile for the camera. These formalities complete you will then be asked a question along the lines of: 'What have you been up to lately?' Unlike any other interview, what you answer to this is of no particular consequence. They are not really interested in your professional experience and still less in details of your domestic life. They will be watching your face rather than listening. You can feel free to invent any exotic adventures you like, within reason of course, brain surgery, for example, might prove a little difficult to account for, should anyone happen to pick up on it. Finally, you will be asked to perform the part. This can be as undemanding as turning to the camera and smiling or entail moves, handling props and dialogue.

Handling props with precision in front of a camera requires more skill than at first seems apparent. Every move must be clear and neat; it's worth going over them in your mind before going into the casting if you are unused to coping with them. Above all remember the product's name must face the camera*. Becoming the character within seconds, as Jill Pearce pointed out in Chapter 1, page 18, also demands skill and concentration but does get easier with practice. The performance over, the camera is turned off and you are dismissed. The whole procedure can last but a few minutes.

In the United States the format is very similar except there are a great many more hopeful actors present and the casting director conducts the session on his or her own. After watching the videos the casting director will shortlist a fortunate few to go through to meet the director. Should the commercial be shown nationwide

*Many actors find working with props difficult and it certainly calls for timing and dexterity. Like any skill it can be learnt. If you feel uncertain of your abilities in this area, spend time at home practising simple tasks, like opening a letter in a few neat movements, lifting a cup and saucer, drinking or replacing the cup in the saucer without a clatter while speaking dialogue, etc., etc.

the repeat fees can amount to a great deal of money. Consequently competition is formidable and the casting can often resemble nothing more than a cattle market. Hold on to your sense of self-worth and let the thought of what a difference all that money could make compensate for any loss of dignity.

As you can see, the process is very businesslike. You are virtually a commodity that may or may not fit the bill. While this obviously doesn't call for the talents of a Meryl Streep or a Daniel Day-Lewis, an appearance in a commercial has often led to an actor being offered a leading role in another branch of the media. Some of the world's best-known directors have made and still make commercials; the casting directors will frequently put someone up for a part in a TV or movie they are working on if they have been impressed with their handling of the commercials casting. So, apart from providing you with a welcome source of income, it can also help you make some useful contacts.

## *Voice-overs*

Of all the work available for an actor on commercials this is perhaps the most sought after. It is a difficult area to break into but if you manage to do so and establish yourself with the commercial companies, the rewards are considerable. As with appearing in a commercial you will receive repeat fees, but in the case of voice-overs, the recording sessions are very intensive but brief so you can do several in a day and fit them in while you are involved with other work. In addition to this the clients don't mind if you have done ads for other products. On the contrary, they seem to prefer to use voices they know or have heard frequently on TV or radio. As a result the same artists tend to get used again and again. This is obviously a very desirable state of affairs for those artists lucky enough to find themselves in that position, but it does make the situation rather like a 'closed shop' for those hoping to follow suit.

So how do you go about getting work in voice-overs and how do you audition? The first step is to make a tape of your work. Remember Chris Sandford's advice given in Chapter 1. Before you start, do your research. Set aside time, at least a week or so, and really listen to commercials on radio and TV. Then tape or record a good sample of them. Listen again and see if there are any that you feel you could do better. These are the ones from which to select the material for your tape, always bearing in mind that you want to show off your versatility, so be sure that you have a variety of material, e.g. straight informative delivery, hard sell, sexy, jokey etc. Also, very importantly, remember the finished tape should last only 3-4 minutes.

You then need to have it professionally recorded. This means approaching a professional recording studio which can be expensive and is getting even more so because many advertising companies have started to demand that an artist's show-reel should be on a CD. This trend is inevitably going to become the norm, so be sure to check with the recording studio what type of reel will be most use to you, as well as how much the session will cost.

Most studio engineers are very helpful and will give tips on how to make your recording sound really professional. Rob Townsend at the well-known recording studio, Angel Sound, also suggests that it be worth while making what is known as a 'reel minute'. This is a separate reel of one minute's duration with 5-10 second excerpts from each of the commercials on your show-reel. This can then be put on CD as a Compilation Disc – a comprehensive sample of your work that shows off the extent of your versatility but doesn't take up more than a minute of the ad executive's time.

This is an example of the invaluable help and advice the studio engineers can give you but it is still important that you have prepared yourself as well as possible before you go into the studio. Remember you are paying for the time.

If you are well rehearsed, know what you are doing and what effects you want to achieve, you can then use the time efficiently and constructively and do your work justice.

The next step is to send your show tape/CD out to the relevant parties. There are agents specialising in voice-overs and many acting agents have a voice-over department, but you can also send your tape directly to the advertising agencies that will (hopefully) employ you. Although they do not make commercials, it is also worth sending a copy to BBC TV as they use voice-over artists for documentary and programme links. There seems to be no such thing as an audition for a voice-over. Most of the work comes through word of mouth, clients liking your work or producers and engineers with whom you have worked recommending you. Even if you have an agent they will only send out your tape to prospective employers. In this instance, their job is to handle any enquiries for your services and collect your repeat fees when they roll in.

## *West End and Broadway plays and major tours*

Appearing in a West End or Broadway theatre production is still one of the most exciting and prestigious engagements for an actor. Even stars are willing to take massive cuts in salary in order to play a tempting part in such a production. Any actor feels a sense of achievement if offered such a part – but the competition for each and every part is great. If you are well known you are approached by the management or your agent suggests you, and a meeting is arranged between you and the director where you may or may not be asked to read, depending on your fame and their preference. For those on the lower rungs of the ladder, the audition process is a little more stressful.

The whereabouts of the audition depends on the management, most of whom have access to West End or other large theatres and the auditions are held there. Failing this, they take place in a hired rehearsal space.

You may or may not receive the script beforehand, depending on whether:

- It's a new play (unlikely).
- It's a revival (more likely).
- A classic (you can get hold of it yourself).

If you haven't a copy of the play it's advisable to arrive at the theatre early enough to look through it thoroughly before auditioning. Half an hour is about right. The difficulty once there is finding somewhere quiet enough to concentrate. The prompt corner is invariably filled with people going about their business rather noisily, or worse still, from the stage you may hear the distinct sound of another actor reading for the same part as you. Resist the temptation to listen, it's disastrous to pick up on someone else's interpretation. When you are handed the script, ask if there is anywhere available where you can read it through alone (the stairway to the dressing rooms is usually a safe bet).

Another word of warning. If for some reason they are running ahead of schedule and ask you to read immediately, don't. Decline politely and insist that you need time to look at the script first. If you refuse in a suitably charming manner, they will soon forget any momentary irritation. But should you let yourself be coerced into reading before you feel ready, all they will remember afterwards is your uncertain performance. You owe it to yourself to be as prepared and confident as you can in the given circumstances.

Should you have had time to work on the script at home and find yourself forced to overhear another auditionee, try to close your ears. Or, if that proves impossible, wait out of earshot until they've finished. So often, hearing someone else's performance makes you question and doubt your own. This is foolish. You can't know what they want and for all you know, you and your own initial response to the part could be 'it'.

Once on stage, go straight to the footlights and greet the people in the auditorium. There may be a scattering of pale faces staring up at you but it is usually the director who addresses you. They will either have a brief discussion with you about the part first or they will ask you to read straight away. If this request takes the form of a gruff command, don't be deterred. It's nothing personal, it could be anything that upset them, from a cold cup of coffee to a drop in the budget. But it can't be you, you haven't done anything yet.

It is common practice for the stage manager or company manager to read with you at this point (you will probably only read with another actor if you are recalled at another date). Stage managers are not actors; they have no ambition to act and they are not trained to sight-read. These observations are made blatantly obvious by the way in which they feed you the lines. Don't be put off. Respond to them as if they were the greatest living actor, delivering your lines in exactly the way you would want them. In other words, take charge of the situation and let your imagination supply you with the ideal co-star.

Use the stage freely, always bearing in mind that they want to see you and not the stage manager, so be careful not to upstage yourself. Be wary of stage directions. It's much safer to ignore them. They will probably be changed anyway during rehearsals. On no account mime props, such as pretending to drink cups of tea, etc. It will detract from your performance, and may look ridiculous. Should you be stopped in mid-flow, do not despair. It doesn't necessarily mean that you were so bad that they couldn't stand another minute, but merely that they've seen enough for the present. After you've finished reading there are a number of possible scenarios that may follow:

- The director may give you notes and work on the scene with you.
- A brief chat and then 'Goodbye'.

- They may ask you there and then to return and read again at a future date.
- A polite but cursory dismissal, for example, 'Thank you, we'll let you know'.
- Silence, except for the rustle of papers and a barely audible murmur from the stalls (this may be accompanied by frantic signals from off stage by the stage management gesturing to you to leave).

However down-hearted you may feel, steel yourself and politely deliver your farewells. Leave the stage with a firm tread and head high (you can always collapse when you're safely outside the stage door).

To be honest, none of these gives any real indication of how successful you've been. Even the last, amazing as it might seem, has been a precursor to a recall and, even on occasions, the offer of a job.

There are some directors who hold, what some might term as, more actor friendly auditions. These either take the form of an improvisation session, from which they short list a number of actors, or just an interview. Both these are nearly always preliminary meetings from which certain actors are selected, given copies of the script and asked to return at a later date. This final audition is usually run along lines similar to those given above but with, of course, the considerable added advantage of having already been able to read the script.

As has been said, the competition for parts is very keen. Even to be given a chance to audition is an achievement. Should you land a part, the thrill you get the first time you see your name and photograph up in front of a theatre on Broadway or in the West End is something you will remember for the rest of your life.

## Major repertory companies

There are so few companies run on the repertory system nowadays that the opportunity to become a member is greatly sought after. To audition you either write off to the company and request one, as suggested by Alison Chard of the RSC in Chapter 1, or your agent organises it. They usually hold auditions once a year and cast for the whole season. This is where your ability to choose and perform an audition speech well is crucial. So, when you are granted an audition, it is worth taking the time to re-read the chapter dedicated to the audition speech. The company may stipulate specific speeches or ask you to choose from given playwrights or certain periods. If not, it is safer to stick to the traditional rule of two contrasting speeches, one straight, one comedy, one of which is classical and the other modern.

The season may include a musical so you may also be asked to prepare a song. Should you have any misgivings about your talent in this field, a word of advice from a dedicated non-singer; in order to come through this experience with some vestige of pride left, invest in some singing lessons so that you gain experience of working with an accompanist. This way you will have a little more confidence when you are confronted with a pianist, an outstretched arm for your music and a request for your preference of key. Remember that you don't have to be a stunning soprano or tenor. There are many instances of actors of, what can only be called, limited musical talent appearing successfully in musicals. Don't be inhibited – have a go.

The venue may vary depending on whether the company is based in or near a city, say London, New York or Los Angeles, or further afield. If their theatre is within easy travelling distance, the audition will be held there. Otherwise the company will hire a rehearsal room. If it's in a theatre the set-up will be similar to that of the West End theatre audition. But in the rehearsal room the auditioner or auditioners (it is usually one at this stage, the director) will sit behind a largish table. In most cases, you will be expected to perform your speeches straight away without any preamble. Approach the table and give your name and brief information about your speeches, i.e. title of plays, playwrights and the name of the parts you'll be playing. If they want to interview you at this stage they will intervene, otherwise go straight into performing your pieces. They may ask to see only one and choose which one of these they prefer. If, however, they leave the choice up to you, although it is sensible to perform the one in which you feel more confident, it is worth noting that after many long hours of watching auditions, viewers have a tendency to react favourably to comedy. Watching endless speeches about gloom, doom and suffering, however effectively portrayed, can be very wearisome and depressing.

When you have finished your speech or speeches you may be asked to do one or all of the following:

- Perform your song.
- Sight-read. This usually involves excerpts from one or all of the plays that they are mounting that season.
- Take part in an interview.

This audition is usually a preliminary one. You generally hear within days whether you are to be recalled or not. At the second audition the artistic director is usually present, on hand to add their input to the final decision. The format will be similar to the previous one but, in this instance, you will certainly be asked to read.

In most cases they will put you out of your misery quite quickly. Should you be successful the experience of working in the repertory system will be invaluable. If not, the audition itself will have provided you with the experience, which is rare today, of performing audition speeches.

## Fringe and equity waivers*

In the last few decades fringe theatre has grown to such an extent that the term hardly applies anymore: it is now an important force in the theatrical world. Not only do productions frequently transfer into mainline theatre but also, it has become, to a large extent, a breeding ground for talent; an outlet for new plays and fledgling directors, as well as providing many actors with their principle source of employment. It is necessary, however, to define the term employment when used in connection with the fringe or Equity Waivers. It has to be faced that as far as the actor is concerned the fee, if there is one, will be minimal. Despite this it is not just the unknown actor that works on the fringe: experienced performers are happy to perform there because the press coverage is excellent and the parts are often more rewarding than those in the other branches of the media. With less money at stake the director is able to put on plays that are adventurous, to take a chance with new actors and to cast the better known ones against type. Such is the status of the fringe nowadays that agents are prepared to send their clients up for it, even though they will receive no commission from the job. They appreciate the value of the experience and exposure gained there. These factors all combine to make competition for the chance to work on the fringe almost as keen as it would be for a job in mainstream theatre.

If you haven't an agent, weekly casting publications such as *Production and Casting Report (PCR)* in the United Kingdom and *Dramalogue* in the United States will inform you of forthcoming productions.

Usually you are asked to send a CV and photograph accompanied by a brief note, but do not presume this

---

*Equity waivers are the American equivalent of some fringe companies, where actors work for nothing or below the lowest salary stipulated by their union, Equity.

will be the case. For example, you may be asked, instead to send off for a questionnaire: so be sure to read the announcement carefully to find out exactly what is required. Getting it wrong can cost you the job before they even read your resumé. They won't even bother to look at your credits.

## CVs, photos and letters

An important word of warning on CVs, photographs and letters. Nothing gives rise to such despair and irritation from casting directors and directors as does the subject of actors' letters. They realise that on occasions like this they are a necessity, but they unanimously plead that they should be brief, typed and to the point. Merely a line stating where you saw the ad and what part you wish to be considered for is quite sufficient. On no account try to be witty, clever or individualist in any way – it will only cause extreme annoyance and end up in the wastepaper bin. The CV should be clearly laid out on one side of one sheet of paper. Should your experience be extensive enough to cover more than a side, limit the choice of credits to the most notable.

Always state the names of the directors you have worked with. Other directors are favourably impressed if you have worked with those whose work they admire. The photograph must be a well-lit head and shoulders shot, of at least postcard size and a good likeness. This last point is of particular importance. It's not a good idea for the actual reality of 'you' to come either as a shock or a disappointment when they meet you.

It is also a waste of money to send photos, CVs etc. to directors 'on spec' just because you've seen their name somewhere. They will almost certainly throw them away. They are inundated with so many that they would need vaults in order to house them all. They have no alternative but to dispose of them unless they are in response to a specific ad.

So, having sent off the perfect photo, CV and brief accompanying note, you will have to wait patiently to see if you get a reply. Unfortunately very few companies have the time or money to let you know if they are not interested and, in this instance, you will only antagonise them if you try to contact them or chase it up in any way. They will contact you if they want you to audition.

## The audition

If the production is in-house, i.e. put on by a company with its own theatre space, the audition will be held there. In the case of a new or independent company, they will have hired a rehearsal room or even in some cases use their own home. This can mean that the playing area varies from small to absolutely minute so bear this in mind when planning the moves for your speeches; keep them adaptable. One actor even found himself auditioning in a corridor.

As is apparent from the above, the kind of company you will audition for may vary widely – from those which have been established for years and are known and respected throughout the profession to the newer companies in the process of building a reputation (running on a shoe-string and putting on plays to attract attention from the press as well as the public), through to a group of actors clubbing together to put on a show in order to give themselves a chance to work. That said, the audition itself is usually quite orthodox, run along similar lines to that of any repertory company; two contrasting speeches (they may only see one but they will want a choice), sight-reading from the proposed play and a short interview. The interview is likely to be more relaxed and casual than usual and in the case of the newly formed theatre company you may well have had more experience in theatre than they have. Don't be misled by this. Companies receive up to five hundred letters per part, they can afford to pick and choose.

Actors have lost opportunities by falling into the trap of patronising the interviewer, hoping to impress them by showing off their superior knowledge and experience. They may listen politely but it's unlikely that you'll get the part. They want to run the show themselves and won't risk the chance of an actor taking over rehearsals and telling them what to do. Another mistake is to approach the interview in too casual a manner, turning up with unkempt hair and clothes of questionable cleanliness or even nursing a hangover from the night before. Both these examples have been tried and tested by a number of young actors and have proved to be very unsuccessful; so learn by their experience.

## The finances

Should you get the job, it's wise to settle the financial arrangements immediately. Leaving it as a casual agreement can lead to ill feeling on both sides later. Obviously, if you have an agent they will handle this for you. If you have to deal with the matter yourself you will need to know whether you are likely to earn anything. Profit share, for example, is open to dispute. It depends very much on how much money has to be paid out weekly to keep the play running and what is the most that can be expected from ticket sales. In many instances even a capacity audience every night would only result in the company breaking even. If this should be the case, then a share is clearly never going to materialise. You may receive expenses but even this is not always feasible. But if you know ahead of time you can budget accordingly. In the United States there are companies where you pay a fee (usually about $40) to join. This covers a season of plays; however you have no guarantee of appearing in all of them or of the size of the parts you will play.

From all this, you can see that nobody goes into the fringe theatre for the money but the opportunities and roles can be good and it can prove a valuable showcase.

Remember the competition, so prepare yourself for the audition with as much care and forethought as you would for any audition. If you get the job it may be the break that you have been waiting for, but even if it's not, the enthusiasm and commitment involved in the production will make it worthwhile.

## Small touring companies

These can provide exciting and prestigious work for actors with the extra bonus of a chance to travel, whether it be the length and breadth of the British Isles or to mainland Europe and beyond. The production varies from company to company. Some, like the renowned Cheek by Jowl, tour a number of plays in repertory with cross casting, others mount single productions and cast each individually.

The audition procedure for both is similar and can be very intensive. A conventional audition (two speeches, short chat) is often only a preliminary to be followed by a week's workshop for those actors who are under consideration. They may 'weed out' yet again at the end of each day but it is more usual to let everyone complete the week before making their final decision.

The workshops are normally eclectic in content, covering movement, improvisation, voice and theatre games besides reading and studying excerpts from the play or plays that are being cast. You may be asked to work in pairs as well as groups. The ability to relate and integrate with other people is of prime importance. The companies are small and for the period of the tour they live virtually in a world of their own. They may play more than one venue in a week. Their members must not only be able to adapt easily to the different sizes and type of stage but also be willing to help out backstage. They must even be ready to take a turn driving the van if necessary. There is no room for prima donnas, the workshops are not just a test of your acting ability, but are also to assess your resourcefulness and adaptability. These companies are the nearest things we have today to the old-fashioned strolling players – a group of people working together as a unit to put on a show.

## T.I.E. (Theatre in Education)

This brand of theatre has features that separate it from any other. Like fringe, it can offer opportunities to unknown actors but unlike it, there is a salary, albeit a small one. Like the aforementioned touring company it travels from place to place but its venues, material, audience and purpose are different. It focuses primarily on people in schools; its aim to entertain but also to educate through drama. The material is usually specially written and each performance is followed by a session with the audience where the content will be discussed and analysed. The production draws on many aspects of theatre besides dialogue, such as mime, music, song and dance in order to hold the attention of its audience and at the same time put the theme across clearly.

Its members have to be able to cope with all this as well as help practically with props, the set, setting up the show beforehand (the get in) and striking it afterwards. This calls for stamina, versatility and a particular sort of talent. The auditions reflect the need to find actors who can fulfil these demands. There are no hard and fast rules as to what the format for these might be. They are usually held in a hired rehearsal room and they generally take the form of a workshop but it is very hard to be specific as to what this might involve. Reports have come back of sessions with tai chi, belly dancing, mine, juggling, gymnastics and Buddhist chanting as well as the more conventional improvisation, with a bit of sight-reading and movement thrown in. Broadly speaking they have a strong bias towards physical theatre. Don't be put off by this even if you have no particular training in this field. Go along ready to have a go at anything. They are not looking for experts but actors who are willing to try, who are open to fresh ideas and above all are enthusiastic. Once again, a friendly manner and a co-operative attitude is required. These are interdependent, tight-knit little groups, so the ability to get on with people, together with a capacity for hard work may well be the deciding factor in getting you the job.

## Role-play for business and institutions

This is a comparatively new source of employment for actors and although it is different in many ways from the more traditional areas of work, it is a growing industry and one that can provide well-paid and satis-fying work for actors. The number of role-play companies and agencies is increasing rapidly all over the country. They use actors on such things as training courses or as an integral part of the job recruitment process. The actor is given a brief by the employer and then has to improvise strictly within these guidelines with a member of the public. In reality this involves playing yourself to a large degree, albeit in alien circum-stances, and interacting with a non-actor. This could be anyone from an employee, to a prospective company manager or a psychiatric patient, so discipline, a sense of responsibility and the ability to keep a clear head are essential qualities for the job. The focus will not be on you and your performance but on their reactions to it. You have to remain constantly aware that there is a lot at stake for those others involved.

The job is clearly not suitable for every actor, demanding as it does considerable 'people skills' and self control. Perhaps because of this, as with voice-overs, work comes usually from word of mouth recom-mendation. There are however, occasional auditions advertised in the trade papers (*PCR*, *SBS* and *The Stage*). These take the form of workshops and, naturally enough, mainly consist of improvisation exercises, acting out given scenarios. Because of the special requirements of the work these workshops can be intensive, so be prepared to spend the day there. Remember these improvisations are quite different in intention to those at an ordinary acting workshop. Here the purpose is to show how real you can be, how well you can stick to your brief and how well you can cope in an awkward situation or with any unexpected behavior from the other participant. Not how inventive you can be or even more undesirably, how well you can 'wrong foot' the other person.

# *Presenting*

## Presenting for TV

Although presenting does not, strictly speaking, come under the category of 'acting', so many acting students decide to take this up at the end of their training rather than follow an acting career, that it seemed sensible to include an account of the usual processes involved in finding work as one. This is not to suggest that acting training is essential to becoming a presenter – in fact the more usual route used to be through journalism.

Recently, with the growth in the number of new TV channels and the growing popularity of magazine programmes, the job of presenter has become more varied and gained a higher profile. Often they are written about in the gossip columns and their names and faces become as well known as a soap or pop star. They have become as important as the programmes they present and many of the skills and talents they require are similar to those used by actors, although of course presenters are called upon to 'act' being themselves. As a result not only are there agencies specialising in handling presenters, but also a number of acting agents who deal with presenting work.

Similarly to voice-overs, the one essential needed to get a job is a very good show-reel. You will need one even to get an agent. As before, research is all important. Try and get yourself as much experience as you can before you make the tape. Learn all you can about the television industry and try to get work with a production company. Get involved with any local opportunities to work before a camera and interview people (e.g. hospital closed-circuit videos). And of course watch other presenters at work, see what you think works and what doesn't and decide which area you think is most suitable for your particular talents, (news-reading, children's, pop, women's programmes etc.).

Unlike the voice-over reel, it is not necessary to have the show-reel professionally produced. A friend's video or camcorder is quite adequate for the job. It's the content that's important. A variety of material is needed: a section straight to camera, a serious interview, a more relaxed one, a vox pox and a section where you are interacting with others. The reel should not last longer than 3 minutes. It is important not to make it any longer – the agent or prospective employer may not play it all the way through and the section they miss might be the very one that would have got you the job or persuaded the agent to take you on.

Once the show-reel is made, send it off to the agents. (The list is in *Contacts*.) You can send it directly to production companies but with the amount of work available from the new independent companies springing up you are likely to make more contacts through an agent.

Your show-reel can get you a job. You can find yourself being hired by a company without them ever meeting you personally. However, this is not always the case and you may be asked to audition.

This will usually consist of a meeting with the producer during which you will be put on camera. This may be while you are having a chat, interacting with others, giving an interview or perhaps presenting material you have previously been asked to prepare. The important thing to remember is that your behaviour off the camera is as important, if not more important, than on. They are watching to see how you behave with others. So much of the success of the job depends on the ability to relax and respond to others, to put them at their ease and to 'be yourself' without affectation and forcing a 'personality'. Try to relax before you go into the meeting. Once in there, concentrate on the other people in the room, be sensitive to their mood, their body language, the tone of their voice and react accordingly.

### Presenting on radio

Unlike radio drama, jobs as a presenter on radio are on the increase. The popularity of commercial radio stations, especially in the regions, has meant that new stations are emerging all the time. Getting started as a presenter, however, can still prove difficult because work is usually obtained by means of word of mouth. Once you have built a reputation or they have heard you on air, radio producers or editors contact you and offer you a slot. Clearly this is going to make getting your first job problematic. Unless you are already broadcasting how are you to become known? The first step then is probably going to be the hardest.

You need to make up a tape of your work to introduce yourself to your prospective employers. The tape has not only to provide them with a sample of your work and to demonstrate your talent and versatility but also to sell 'you'. To give them a reason to offer you the work rather than somebody else. So before you rush out and make it, be sure you are really ready to do so. Get as much experience as you can beforehand. Grab any chance you can to interview people, to DJ and find an opportunity to broadcast on amateur radio shows. This way you will not only gain valuable experience but also begin to find your own strengths and weaknesses, what you enjoy and what you find more difficult. You must then decide what area of broadcasting you want to focus on. Research that area thoroughly. Listen to other broadcasters, analyse their style, decide on your own. Then practice, practice, practice until you feel confident that you are ready to make a tape that will show you off at your best.

The tape should last about 3-5 minutes. But you want to be sure that the first 30 seconds really grabs their interest and makes them want to play it all. Although you are focusing on a particular area, be versatile within it. Vary the types of 'phone-in' interviews and how you handle them. Don't be too narrow in your choice of music. When you are happy with your tape send it off to as many producers and editors as possible working in your chosen area.

# 6

## Conclusions and Observations

Well there it is. An examination of all the various methods, procedures and formulas the employers from every branch of the media have dreamt up to find a foolproof but fair way of finding the 'right actor for the job'. They clearly haven't succeeded. How could they when the outcome is always dependent on that most unreliable arbiter of excellence, opinion. You will have come to realise, from reading the book, that so many of the final decisions are influenced by the mood, attitude and compatibility of the people involved. A role can be cast on a whim or can be lost because of a cup of cold coffee. But until a genius comes up with a better idea you are stuck with the system, imperfect as it is. In order to survive you need resilience and confidence. The previous chapters will have told you what to expect and how to handle it. This will give you confidence but you will still have to find a way of withstanding the inevitable rejections and disappointments that are an integral part of the profession.

Of course, it's not all gloom and doom, there are great compensations. The work itself can be rewarding, stimulating and exciting. Actors, for the most part, are friendly, supportive fellow workers. Few other professions provide you with the camaraderie that you get when working with a company or on location with a film, but the times in between can seem long and depressing. By now you will have come to recognise how vital it is that you approach every interview with a firm sense of respect for yourself and your talent. Unless you are one of the lucky few, and there are only a very few who work continuously, this is difficult to sustain. In order to do this you need to find a way of fulfilling and enjoying your life when you're not working. Apart from anything else, as anyone will tell you who has experienced a stormy relationship or long periods out of work, watching the telephone is a sure way to guarantee it won't ring.

There are all the usual suggestions, attend classes, go to see other people's work, start a hobby, etc. – all excellent but they often end up being just a way of filling in time rather than something that really involves and interests you. And they often cost money. The financial issue cannot be dismissed – starving in a garret may be a romantic notion but the reality can be damaging to your health and self-esteem. On the other hand, endless periods of bar work or waitressing can be equally demoralising. What is wanted is an occupation that provides you with an income, an interest and yet enables you to take time off to attend auditions. Too good to be true? Maybe. Unless you take matters into your own hands, start up your own business, perhaps with a group of other actors, one where the allocation of hours can be controlled and adapted. A service company of some sort, for example. A shopping service, where you would undertake the weekly visits to the supermarket for wealthy professional couples. Yes, there are people who will pay: target the affluent areas of the city. A sandwich business, serving either office blocks or from your own stall. Catering for formal dinners, organising children's parties – mind you that calls for a strong constitution! There are many more possibilities. Think of all the tasks that people have to perform when they get home from work, at night or at the weekend, when they would much rather be sitting with their feet up relaxing.

You will be surprised how many are willing and able to pay for it. If you run the company with other actors you can cover for each other when you need to go to castings or when you get an acting job. You will also have access to the actor's greatest and most valuable source of research – the public.

If you prefer to work alone, consider taking an evening course in a subject or skill that interests you with a view to earning some money from it eventually. The point is not to feel threatened by taking up another occupation besides acting. It doesn't mean that you've given up, or that you've failed or that you'll never work again as an actor. Quite the contrary. Think of those actors who famously run successful business ventures as a sideline. Paul Newman and his sauces, Jane Asher's cakes, Arnie's, Sly's and Bruce's Planet Hollywood and the list could go on. In fact knowing the way life works, you will probably be inundated the moment the new business starts off. It can also provide you with the means to pay for acting classes and theatre tickets. As long as you continue to work on your audition speeches and join a play-reading group or something similar, you won't feel cut off from the profession.

When you attend interviews and auditions you will have an air of achievement and self-belief rather than desperation. You will be in a position of having some control over your own destiny, or as Thelma Holt put it, 'You will know that you have a choice'. You are not begging for a job but considering one.

In the same vein, if you have been out of work for a long period or have become typecast and the parts you are offered are undemanding and unrewarding, take charge of the situation. Start your own company. Mount your own production, either on your own or with some fellow actors. It can be done. The fringe is full of people who have raised money on just that. Not only are you providing yourself with work, a chance of publicity and recognition, your own choice of material, but also a valuable insight into how it feels to be in a position of hiring rather than being hired.

Whether you decide to take this advice or not, realise that its purpose is to ensure that you don't become a victim of the profession's unreliability. This book can give you all the necessary information and techniques to succeed in interviews and auditions. There is only one other factor to consider. The importance of sustaining a sense of self-worth. They say that 'Success is a state of mind'. Maybe it would be more accurate to say success can be achieved by a state of mind.

# 7

# *Suggested Audition Pieces*

Here is a short list of effective but less frequently performed audition speeches. This may prove particularly helpful for the Shakespeare, as it is often difficult to find a speech that hasn't been 'overdone'. There are many books that deal specifically with audition speeches and it is well worth browsing through them. If you are good at writing, originating your own material is also a consideration. But if you decide to do so it would be wise to seek feedback from an honest and discerning source before performing it at an audition.

## Shakespeare

### *Female*

*Henry IV Part I*, Act II, Scene III
Lady Percy: 'O, my good lord! why are you thus alone?...And I must know it, else he loves me not.'

*Henry IV Part II*, Act II, Scene III
Lady Percy: 'O yet for God's sake, go not to these wars!...Have talk'd of Monmouth's grave.'

*Henry V*, Act II, Scene III
Mistress Quickly: 'Nay, sure he's not in hell...as cold as any stone.'

*Cymbeline*, Act III, Scene II
Imogen: 'Who? thy lord? that is my lord. Leonatus...Twixt hour and hour?'

*Cymbeline*, Act III, Scene II
Imogen: 'I false?...Do his bidding strike.'

*The Comedy of Errors*, Act II, Scene II
Adriana: 'Ay, Ay Antipholus, look strange and frown...I live dis-stained, thou, undishonoured.'

## *Male*

*Henry IV Part I*, Act I, Scene III
Hotspur: 'My liege, I did deny no prisoners...Betwixt my love and your high majesty.'

*Henry IV Part II*, Act IV, Scene IV
Prince Hal: 'Why doth the crown...Will I do to thine leave, as tis left to me.'

*Cymbeline*, Act II, Scene II
Iachimo: 'The crickets sing, and man's o'er-labour'd sense...Though this a heavenly angel, hell is here.'

*Henry V*, Act III, Scene II
Boy: 'As young as I am...and therefore I must cast it up.'

*The Two Gentlemen of Verona*, Act II, Scene III
Launce: 'Nay, 'Twill be this hour ere I have done weeping...but see how I lay the dust with my tears.'

*'Love's Labour's Lost*, Act III, Scene I
Biron: 'O! – and I, forsooth, in love!...Some men must love my lady, and some Joan.'

## Modern

### *Female*

*Random Moments in a May Garden,* James Saunders
Anne: 'Katie and Anne, two little girls...Staring at his ridiculous moustache.'

*Virginia*, Edna O'Brien
Virginia: Eros comes on dirty wings...the world belongs to men.

*Laughing Wild,* Christopher Durang
Woman: 'Have you all wondered why sexual intercourse sometimes makes you want...Laugh and you...Cry alone later.'

*Smelling a Rat*, Mike Leigh
Melanie-Jane Beetles: 'I like this flat, it's gorgeous...Can I have a cup of tea?'

*Savoury Meringue*, James Saunders
Hessian: 'I had this bloke. Six years, six years I had him round...I'm sick of it, I'm not really.'

*Demi-God,* Richard LaGravenese
Woman: 'I know you're going to go...that feels much better.'

*Henceforward*, Alan Ayckbourn
Zoe: 'Well, here I am...I'll be as quick as I can. I'm so sorry.'

## Male

*The Public Eye*, Peter Shaffer
Julian: 'My name is Cristoforou...They ease the heart.'

*Class Enemy*, Nigel Williams
Rakes: 'My ol' man 'e Lives...Thas' is a garden innit.'

*Rosencrantz and Guildenstern are Dead*, Tom Stoppard
Rosencrantz: 'It's silly to be depressed...time is its only measure.'

*Luther*, John Osborne
Tetzel: 'Are you wondering who I am...this concerns you.'

*The Faith Healer*, Brian Friel
Teddy: 'Okay. We head down into the valley...Village of Kinlochbervie.'

*Chips with Everything*, Arnold Wesker
Pip: 'One day, when I was driving...chips with everything.'

*Quartermaine's Terms*, Simon Gray
Meadle: 'Oh, the usual combination of unexpected...Does it still show?'

*Total Eclipse*, Christopher Hampton
Verlaine: 'My mother had three miscarriages...smashed the jars.'

# 8

# *Suggested Material for Sight-reading Practice*

**Children's books**   Read aloud to any child you can persuade to listen. They are brutally honest yet receptive audiences. *Winnie the Pooh, Alice in Wonderland* and *The Wind in the Willows* are really children's books for adults. Don't attempt them until you feel confident and have practised for a while on less demanding texts.

**Magazine ads**   These really force you to use your voice freely.

**Romantic novels**   The more purple the prose, the more fun you can have.

**Charles Dickens** (any)   Quite demanding but full of wonderful characters to experiment with.

**Jane Austen and George Bernard Shaw**   Both are excellent training for keeping the sense going to the end of seemingly endless sentences.

**Christopher Marlowe and Edmund Spenser**   An opportunity to develop and indulge in playing with imagery and the sensuality of words.

**Shakespeare** The best – especially verse, the text is so dense with meaning and the structure of the verse such that you have to find the changes of pace, emotion and thought.

Raid second-hand bookshops and charity shops for inexpensive copies of plays. Buy anything even if you've never heard of it; you might make some exciting discoveries.

# 9

# *Three Simple Relaxation Exercises*

These three exercises are straightforward, easy and practical – the first is done lying down, the second standing and the third, walking. While the first two require a little time and, to begin with, privacy, the last can be practised as you walk along the street. Although the exercises are very simple in theory it may take you some time before you can perform them without loss of concentration. Be patient with yourself. In this instance the endeavour is of value in itself. If you worry about doing the exercises successfully, you won't!

## Exercise 1

Lie on your back on the floor (I'm afraid a bed won't do). Make sure you are as comfortable as possible – some people prefer to lie in the Alexander 'supine' position, i.e. head resting on a book, knees bent, feet flat on the floor, arms by your side – but this is not essential. Rock your head from side to side a few times to free the muscles at the back of the neck. Make sure the chin is not tipped too far back, the front of the throat should feel soft.

Close your eyes. Take your attention down to your feet – wriggle your toes then clench them tightly. Hold them like that while you count up to five. Let go. Enjoy the feeling of release for a moment, then tense the muscles in the foot and hold for a count of five before letting go. Again take time to appreciate the two different sensations. Repeat the same routine with the calf muscles.

Proceed slowly up through the body, tightening and releasing the muscles. The thighs, the buttocks, the back and the waist (press down against the floor, then release), the abdomen, the shoulder blades, hunch the shoulders up, and release down, the upper arm, the forearm, the hands. Then move up to the face. Grit the teeth, let go, screw up your nose, let go, clench the eyes closed, let go, lastly furrow the brow and release.

Lie quietly for a few moments after which take your attention down to the feet again. Imagine that with each inward breath you are drawing up energy through your body. Take your time. With each intake of breath imagine the energy rising further up through your body until you feel filled with it, ready for action but without anxiety or restless impatience. Give yourself time to enjoy this sensation.

When you are ready to get up go slowly through the following sequence of actions. Cover your face with your hands. Open your eyes into the palms of your hands so the light is soft and filtered. Gently rock your head to and fro a couple of times. Lower your hands and hug your knees into your chest. Hold the position for a minute then rock the body from side to side so that the back of the waist is massaged against the floor. Roll over onto your side and slowly get up. It is important to take your time coming out of this relaxation, otherwise you will undo the benefit you have derived from it.

## Exercise 2

This exercise also requires a little time. Stand with your feet approximately shoulder distance apart with your knees relaxed. Take your attention down to your feet.

Notice whether your weight is mainly on your heels or your toes. Rock gently backwards and forwards feeling the shift of weight. Find a point where the weight is balanced centrally over the arches of the foot. Check that your legs are still relaxed; if they have tightened release the knees and return to the point of balance over the arches of the feet.

Next roll the right foot over towards the instep then towards the outside of the foot. Find the central point of balance between the two. Repeat with the left foot. Now your weight should be centrally balanced over the arches of the foot. Sway slightly to and fro to ensure you have achieved this as far as possible and that the legs are still relaxed. When you are satisfied with the position take a few steps, stop and see if you can return to this point of balance. Adjust your weight if necessary.

Take your attention up to the pelvis and follow a similar series of actions. Tilt the pelvis first of all backwards and forwards until you find the point at which the weight is balanced centrally over the arches of the feet, then tilt it from side to side until the weight is again balanced evenly at the central point. Repeat the process with your shoulders and finally your head. When you feel that your body is aligned and balanced over the centre of your feet, check that the legs and arms are free from tension, then take your attention to the top of your head.

Imagine that the sun is shining way above you and you are growing towards it. Imagine its gentle warmth radiating down filling you with energy. Take your attention down to your feet. Imagine you have roots growing from the soles of your feet deep into the ground. Feel how the ground supports you. Draw energy from it into your feet and up through your body. Energy is coming to you from above and below. Let yourself experience and enjoy the sensation for a while. Then when you feel ready, walk around a little, stop and see if you can return to your point of balance. See if you can return to it at times during the rest of the day.

## Exercise 3

The final exercise is simple and fun. Only one word of warning: DON'T BUMP INTO ANYTHING. You really have to concentrate on your surroundings.

Take a walk, even a stroll to the shops will do, as long as it takes at least a quarter of an hour.

Spend the first 5 – 10 minutes (depending on how long you have planned to walk) noticing everything about your surroundings that are happening below your waist level. The next 5 – 10 minutes notice only things that are going on from waist level up to eye level. Finally notice only things that are above and at eye level.

Do watch out for kerbs, traffic lights, etc. – but in fact once you've done it once or twice you'll find you will deal with all these hazards with ease.

This exercise not only relaxes the mind by giving it specific tasks, rather than letting it dwell on its usual worries, but also improves your powers of concentration, a valuable asset for any actor.

# *Index*

accents 16, 25, 32, 67
acting classes 25, 113
actor's co-operatives 16
agents 16, 17, 49, 79, 80, 89, 90, 95, 98
Alexander Technique 56
Angel Sound 94
Annett, Paul 26
appearance 12, 15, 17, 18, 24, 53, 54, 89
approach to texts 35-8, 59-66
auditions 10, 12, 27, 30-42, 73-9, 92, 95-7, 99, 102
audition speeches 10, 27, 30-42, 74, 95, 105, 116-19
awkard situations 49, 50, 51

Bartlett, Carolyn 9
beginning and ending speeches 39
Bidmead, David 12, 54
*Brideshead Revisited* 24
Broadway 92
*Brother Cadfael* 22
Brown, Angie 20

Cameron, Sarah 20
Capaldi, Peter 26
casting 11, 13, 14, 18, 22, 23, 26, 79-103
    directors, 11, 16, 19, 20, 23, 47, 48, 50, 79, 81, 82, 84, 85, 86, 87, 92
    publications, 25, 79
    sessions, 29, 79-103

chanting 103
Chard, Alison 14, 95
Chasin Agency 15
Cheek by Jowl 105
choosing a song 74, 75, 76
choosing a speech 10, 27, 30-4, 74, 98, 116-19
classes 25, 113
classical speeches 33, 95, 116-17
clothes 13, 16, 17, 18, 19, 20, 24, 53, 54
commercial castings 19, 90-3
confidence 52, 72, 104, 106, 107
controlling nerves 55, 68, 69, 70, 71, 78, 113-16
coping with rejection 57
C.V.s 12, 102-3

delivery of the speech 15, 27, 39
directors 11, 13, 14, 44, 45, 47, 49, 50, 54, 81, 82, 84, 85, 87, 88, 90, 92, 93, 95, 99, 101, 102
drama
    colleges, 9, 11, 12, 25, 29, 73-9
    schools, 9, 11, 12, 25, 29, 73-9
*Dramalogue* 101
drama auditions
    college, 73-9
    school, 73-9
drying 34, 41

Etcetera Theatre 12, 54
exits 21, 41, 55

film
    castings, 83-9
    directors, 18, 26, 44, 45, 50,
        84, 85, 87, 88, 92
    interviews, 16, 17, 83, 89
films, for home market 88, 89
fluffs 66
fringe and Equity Waiver audi-
    tions 16, 101-5
fringe theatre 12, 16, 25, 101-5

Gordon, Janey 19
Guildhall School of Music and
    Drama 9
gymnastics 106

Hands, Terry 27
Hawthorne, Nigel 23
Help, Audrey 15
Hill, Serena 20
Holt, Thelma 22, 28, 52, 114
Hussein Waris 17, 46

I, Claudius 23
I.D.s on camera 90
improvisation 76, 77, 95, 106
interviews 10, 11, 15, 18, 20,
    22, 23, 26, 29, 43-57, 77,
    78, 80, 81, 83-92, 95, 97,
    100, 105
    technique, 43-57

Jarrott, Charles 16
Jarrott, Suzanne 15
Jones, Albi 10
Jones Doreen 24, 49, 83
Jones, Wyn 9
juggling 106

keywords 37
layout of text 62

learning speech 34
leaving,
    drama college, 14, 25
    drama school, 14, 25
length of speeches 31
letters 12, 98
low budget movies 87

major repertory theatre audi-
    tions 98-100
major tour auditions 105-6
Middlesex University 11
mime 106
modern speeches 37, 95, 117-
    19
movement 11, 37, 99, 106-7
movies, for home market 87,
    88
musical accompaniment 76, 99

nerves 21, 22, 25, 46, 55, 68,
    69, 70, 71, 78, 122-5
nervous tension 55, 68, 69, 70,
    71, 122-5

PAs 81
PCR 101-108
Pearce, Jill 18, 92
personal assistant see PA
Peters, Fraser & Dunlop 15
photographs 14, 16, 17, 25, 98,
    99, 101-3
physicality 12, 37, 54, 106-7
pilot season 83
Poldark 26
preparation 16, 18, 20, 24, 28,
    49
presenters 20, 108-11
presenting
    presenting for TV 108-10
    presenting on radio 110,
        111
presenting a speech 10, 27, 39-41
Prime Suspect 24, 26

producers 45, 81, 83, 84, 85
props 32, 91

questionnaires 101
questions and answers 20, 46, 48, 53

radio 19, 89, 90, 110, 111
radio drama 89, 90
relaxation techniques 56, 68, 69, 70, 71, 122-5
repertory companies 16, 99-100
research 16, 24, 49
Robinson, Matthew 16, 80
Roleplay 20, 107, 108
Royal National Theatre 20
Royal Shakespeare Company 14, 27, 95
Rubin, Leon 11
rudeness 18, 22, 45, 49, 51, 52

Sandford, Chris 19
screen tests 85
Secret Army 26
Sherlock Holmes 9, 26
show-reels 19, 93-5, 108-11
sides 80
singing 74, 75, 76, 96
Slight, Sweetpea 22
small touring companies 105-6
smoking 12, 55
speeches to avoid 31
Spotlight 16, 25
stage directions 66
staging the speech 13, 27, 40, 99
suggestions for,
    audition speeches 116-19
    sight-reading, 120-1

Tai-chi 103

techniques of sight-reading 59-68
television
    casting, 79-83
    directors, 18, 22, 26, 44, 45, 50, 81, 82
    interviews, 16, 17, 80-3
theatre directors 11, 13, 14, 23, 41, 44, 45, 50, 93, 95, 99, 102
theatre games 10
Theatre in Education (T.I.E.) 106-107
theatre producers 28
Tomba Theatre Company 10
Touring companies 105-6

United Kingdom
    commercial castings, 90
    film castings, 84-9
    television castings, 80
United States
    commercial castings, 92, 93
    film castings, 85
    television castings, 82
using the playing area 40, 94, 99
using words to good effect 10, 37, 63, 64

Vincent, Maureen 15
vocal usage 38, 67
voice 38, 67, 102
voice-overs 19, 93-5

weekly casting publications 25, 79, 98
West End productions 95-8
Wise, Herbie 23, 82
working on a speech 34-41
workshops 105
'W' questions 35, 60